A Faith of a Different Color

Honest Lessons on Trusting God in Real Life

MICHELLE MERRIN

CROSSBOOKS

CrossBooks™
A Division of LifeWay
1663 Liberty Drive
Bloomington, IN 47403
www.crossbooks.com
Phone: 1-866-879-0502

First published by CrossBooks 10/3/2011

ISBN: 978-1-4627-0649-5 (sc)
ISBN: 978-1-4627-0650-1 (hc)
ISBN: 978-1-4627-1052-2 (e)

Library of Congress Control Number: 2011916371

Printed in the United States of America

This book is printed on acid-free paper.

Contents

Preface

I've wanted to write a book for a long time now. I've thought and re-thought what it would be about and what it would look like for what seems like an eternity. I've written down little bits, taken notes, and made plans for over twenty years. All of the ideas were tucked away and prayed over, saved for "someday". Several times throughout those years, God confirmed to me that indeed I would write a book sometime in the future. Finding his perfect timing was the key . . . and so I waited expectantly.

But this is not the book I planned to write. In fact, it's not even close. The subject matter is completely different, and quite frankly it's a book I never wanted to write. I certainly never wanted the experiences that have allowed me to write this book. But it's the book God planned for me to write.

I've known for a long time that God's ways are not the same as my ways. I've even been able to accept that on a fairly regular basis most of my life. You see, faith was always easy for me. I'm not exactly sure of all of the reasons for that, but I came to the realization at some point that faith was a gift that God had given me. In fact, I believed with incredible certainty that faith was one of my God-given spiritual gifts, and so I gave him all the credit for it. It wasn't that my life had been so easy that faith was not an issue. As you will read in the pages ahead, I had faced many challenges in life; and God had grown my faith in numerous situations throughout the years.

But, in the midst of one particularly challenging and long-term trial, I reached a point spiritually that I had never been before . . . a place where faith was not enough (or at least MY faith was not enough). As God and I wrestled for months and the enemy did his very best to destroy me, I faced more and more places where I had never been before. And, just when I believed the struggle was finally over, the months turned into years. The darkness was at times overwhelming, and I have to admit that the enemy had many victories. But he did not win the battle because God did not allow him to. And, through the interaction of God's Word with my experience, I now know things about God and the life of faith that I didn't know before. Or at least I learned how to move the things I knew about God and the life of faith from *head* knowledge to *heart* knowledge—the kind of knowledge that really makes a difference every day. This book is about sharing some of those truths with you and letting God use my experiences to minister to you. I decided to use a Bible study format because I believe in the power of God's Word to transform lives whether studied on our own or with a group of other believers. This book is suitable for either.

Maybe someday I'll still write the book I originally planned, but for now this is the one God has given me. I am not an expert; God works in each person uniquely, and I only know what he's done in *my* life. But my prayer is that he has directed you to read this book for a specific purpose and that his words through me will be exactly what you need to hear right now. I started praying for you when I started writing this book, and I am still praying for you as you read it. One thing I know for sure: God works in ways you and I can't even imagine, so I am confident that he has brought us together at this moment in time for his perfect purposes. To God be the glory!

Michelle Merrin
2011

Acknowledgements

My wonderfully patient and supportive prayer warrior husband, Ron—thank you for encouraging me to write, for always believing in me, and for always allowing me the space to become what God intended me to be through every stage of our life together. You can still make me laugh after all these years. You are a true blessing, and your constant love is an amazing gift from God.

Scott and Brad, my precious sons—it is a profound privilege to be your mother. Our honest relationship and your commitment to walk with God on a daily basis bring me great joy. Thank you for your encouragement and prayers for this project.

Laura—the newest member of our family and my only daughter so far. I am very grateful for our relationship and the challenge of a fresh perspective within our home. You are God's gift not only to Scott but to our entire family.

My parents, Leonard and Margo Williams—you laid the foundation for my faith and provided the atmosphere for it to grow. Thank you for your example of a faithful marriage and your desire to walk with God throughout your lives. I miss you, Dad.

Ginger—your unconditional love has made a huge difference in my life. I can always count on you to listen intently, validate me, and hold me accountable with your challenging words. I always look forward to our stimulating conversations and am very grateful for your honesty, your prayers, and the gift from God that you are to me.

My dear lifelong friend, Karen—what a precious gift God gave to me that first day of 7th grade band so many years ago! Thank you for your constant encouragement and support and for providing a covering of prayer for me in this endeavor. Your role was absolutely essential, and I am truly grateful.

My other partners in prayer for this project, Randy and Cathy— thank you for joining me on this journey! I am confident that your prayers kept me in step with God's Word as I wrote.

Our family at Mt. View Church—when we started attending, our greatest needs were for healing and to be fed spiritually, and we are grateful to Pastor Bill and all the others who provided a safe and Biblical environment where God could do his work in us.

Tom Barwick, my youth pastor through most of my junior high and high school years—I can still remember your insistence on defining faith in practical terms that made sense to a teenager without sacrificing an emphasis on the equal importance of truth and distinctive Christian living. You made a difference in helping me to connect all the dots.

My first Religion professor at college (a Mahayana Buddhist)—God used his extensive knowledge coupled with a lack of Biblical faith to teach me about the importance of faith and the role it plays in my spiritual walk.

My unconventional freshman English professor, who believed in my ability to write and encouraged me to pursue it—God used the obvious absence of absolute truth and all of its ramifications in his life to teach me to love truth and value it above all else.

Authors and books that have had a significant impact on my developing faith:

Eugene Peterson—He is my favorite; and (although not equal in either knowledge or experience) I feel as though we are kindred spirits (after all, we *did* graduate from the same college!). I am always anxious to read the next book.

Beth Moore—*Get Out of That Pit, Praying God's Word*

Katie Brazelton—*Pathway to Purpose for Women*

Rick Warren—*The Purpose Driven Life*

Charles Colson—*Loving God, How Now Shall We Live*

Pete Greig—*God On Mute*

J.I. Packer—*Knowing God*

Michael Card—numerous songs and writings

Lesson 1

What's Faith Got to Do With It?

Everything in life is about faith and trust. Some who are more science-oriented than I am might disagree. They would tell me that there are certain things that can be proven and therefore do not require faith. But even science is a collection of theories that must be believed. And, although many theories are now considered to be truth in the twenty-first century and many scientific theories have been "proven" to be explanations of how things are or how things operate a majority of the time, they are still theories developed by man and subject to human error. Hence, they require faith and trust.

We can apply this idea to the familiar example of a chair. Every time we sit in one, we expect it to hold us up. We expect this based on past experience with chairs, the law of gravity, the ratio of our weight to the size of the chair, etc. So we say we can be "certain" that the chair will hold us up. But we can never be completely certain until we sit in this particular chair on this particular day whether we will remain upright or end up on the floor.

What are some other examples of everyday living that require faith? What about the days, the months, the seasons? We have come to trust in these patterns and even predict the weather, the sunrise, the sunset, and other aspects of the natural order with relative certainty. Yet we cannot *cause* these things but can only have faith (based on past experience and scientific research of these phenomena) that they will continue to occur in the same way in the future.

Another example is relationships with other people. All relationships require trust because each of us can really only control our *own* actions. We marry based on trust that our spouse will remain faithful, and we share our feelings and thoughts with our friends based on the degree to which we trust them to guard the information and thereby uphold our trust in them. A relationship without faith and trust is not a true relationship; it lacks the basic ingredients to make it function properly.

Most Christians are familiar with Hebrews 11, also known as the "faith chapter". The first verse of this chapter describes faith as the "fundamental fact of existence . . . the firm foundation under everything that makes life worth living . . . our handle on what we can't see" (MSG). Other versions use such words as "assurance, conviction" (NASB), "being sure, certain" (NIV), and "proof, perceiving as real fact" (AMP). According to this verse, faith is an essential element of all of our lives; and it is also very near to fact or truth. Of course, that depends on what we place our faith in.

Our trust in anything is based on what we know about that thing and what our past experience has been with it. Trust is also affected by the experiences of others and the stories they tell us about a particular thing. Most people came to believe that the world is round based not on their own experiences but on the experiences of the explorers who were willing to venture into the unknown based on faith alone. What we now know to be a fact (after seeing photos from space) was for many centuries something that had to be taken on faith.

Likewise, our trust in God is based on what we know about him, what our past experience with him has been, or the experiences of others. The more we know about God, the stronger our faith in him becomes. As we discover and experience his character traits that are unlike the character traits of anyone else we know, we begin to have a perspective on faith that resembles the words from Hebrews 11:1—a firm foundation, assurance, certain.

But not everyone's faith will look the same. I have found that God teaches each of us different parts of himself at different times and in different ways. Where we are in the walk of faith and what our faith looks like directly relates to what God is teaching us through our experiences and his Word. The one thing that ties all of us together in our faith is its foundation in truth, which along with God himself is unchanging.

The object of faith is truth as revealed in Jesus Christ, the incarnation of God's Word. And, to those of us who exist after Christ's incarnation, truth is also revealed in God's written Word: the Bible. Our faith is directly related to how well we know God through our relationship with Christ and our knowledge of Scripture.

When Christ was here on earth, he challenged us to have faith like little children. When I was first married, I taught preschool in a church daycare for a couple of years. After my own children were born, I continued for several years to teach preschool Sunday school classes. What I liked best about teaching that age was the unwavering trust that these little ones placed in me simply because I was their teacher. And, as they got to know me better throughout the school year, they trusted me even more as they learned that I was trustworthy. They believed everything I said to be the gospel truth, and for the most part they obeyed my rules without questioning them. It was easy to teach new concepts to them because they trusted what I told them and were eager to follow as I helped them to learn new skills and gain more knowledge.

This is the childlike faith that Christ referred to and the kind of faith he wants us to have. This is not a child*ish* faith, which Paul addressed in 1 Corinthians 13:11 and encouraged us to "put away". Instead, this faith is *like* that of a child, who believes easily (Santa Claus, the Tooth Fairy, and the Easter Bunny prove that!), doesn't always question before obeying, and hasn't yet learned to apply reason to everything, therefore muddying the waters of faith and trust. Children show us that there is a direct correlation between belief and behavior. What we believe has everything to do with how we behave.

What if we could all trust God's truth in the same way that children trust? What would this look like? How would our lives change if we truly believed what God has said to us in his Word and operated every aspect of our lives on faith, trusting God in the same way that the rest of his creation does? Worry is the opposite of trust, and Matthew 6:25-30 reminds us that only humans struggle with faith:

> "That is why I tell you not to worry about everyday life—whether you have enough food and drink, or enough clothes to wear. Isn't life more than food, and your body more than clothing? Look at the birds. They don't plant or harvest or store food in barns, for your heavenly Father feeds them. And aren't you far more valuable to him than they are? Can all your worries add a single moment to your life? And why worry about your clothing? Look at the lilies of the field and how they grow. They don't work or make their clothing, yet Solomon in all his glory was not dressed as beautifully as they are. And if God cares so wonderfully for wildflowers that are here today and thrown into the fire tomorrow, he will certainly care for you. Why do you have so little faith?" (NLT)

In matters of faith, I want to resemble little children and the rest of God's creation rather than modeling the characteristics of grown-up humans. The longer I walk with God, it seems the easier it should be to have a strong faith that grows and conquers doubt regularly. But this isn't always the case, and sometimes we find ourselves in the middle of life circumstances that cause us to struggle in our faith and to doubt what we have learned in the past. After all, "life is hard, and it might not get easier".[1]

This book is about being honest in our walk of faith and moving toward a place where faith and trust rule our lives more often than worry and doubt. As I have learned over the past forty-eight years in relationship with God, struggling in our faith doesn't mean we're not on track with God regardless of what some fellow people of faith might want us to believe. Does your struggle move you closer to God? If it does, then it's ordained by him and a positive thing. Job's story in the Old Testament is a perfect example of this.

This book is intended to encourage you in specific faith issues as you "continue to work out your salvation . . . for it is God who works in you" (Philippians 2:12-13, NIV), for "he who began a good work in you will carry it on to completion" (Philippians 1:6, NIV). Let God do his work in each circumstance of your life. In the end, you will be glad you did.

According to Matthew 18:1-4, what are the two important characteristics of children that God wants our faith to look like? _____

_____

Look at Matthew 6:25-30 again. What do the birds and flowers model for us about trust? _____

_____

_____

What has been your easiest time of trusting God so far? _____

_____

_____

What has been your most difficult time of trusting God so far? ___

_____

_____

Read 2 Corinthians 5:7 and 4:18. What does it mean to walk by faith and not by sight? _____

_____

_____

Read 1 Peter 1:3-9. According to these verses, what is the purpose of trials and suffering for Christians? _____

_____

_____

Read Hebrews 11:1-12:4. How do these examples of faith specifically encourage you today in your walk of faith? _____

_____

_____

How does Jesus' example encourage you? _____

_____

_____

_____

_____

_____

Lesson 2

Trusting God's Word

The first step that is necessary in a journey of faith is a decision regarding what to put your faith in. This may sound fundamental and elementary, but it is essential.

If we are seeking to know God and discover a basis for our faith, it seems obvious that we will look to God's Word, the Bible, to determine how to do just that. But reading the Bible and gaining more knowledge about God, though vitally important, is only part of the equation. As I discovered firsthand during my freshman year of college, what we believe *about* the Bible is just as important as the knowledge we have *of* the Bible. In other words, knowledge and faith go hand in hand.

My "Major World Religions" class was taught by an engaging and scholarly professor during my first semester away from home. He told us in detail all of the doctrines and practices of Judaism, Christianity, Hinduism, and Buddhism, choosing to conceal his own beliefs from us until the end of the class. With each different religion, I was impressed with his knowledge and convinced that this man believed what he was teaching. When he revealed after fifteen weeks that he was a Mahayana Buddhist, I was amazed. For the first time in my life, I had met someone who understood Christianity and God's Word completely yet lacked the faith necessary to put that knowledge into practice. Later that year, another professor taught me a lesson about truth. As his lifestyle and words modeled the complete absence of absolute truth, I came to realize the vital role of truth in a believer's life and walk. Together, these men inadvertently helped to make faith and truth important distinctive marks of my walk with God.

According to Unger, faith and truth are intertwined. Faith is required for salvation; but, once saved, we also experience faith as a *result* of salvation.[1] It takes faith to believe and be convicted of truth, and faith trumps reason without opposing it. In other words, even though faith has the final say, it is based on something that is reasoned or reasonable: the unchanging and completely truth-full Word of God. But how do we reach a point where God's truth becomes the object of our faith and what we base our lives on? If knowing God better affects the growth of our faith, where do we go to learn more about him? And what do we need to believe about the Bible in order for that process to begin?

There are many verses in the Bible that help us to understand and believe that it is not an ordinary book. Starting in the Old Testament, let's look at a few of these passages and discover why we can trust God's Word.

Look up these verses and write what words are used to describe God's Word:

Psalm 18:30 _____

Psalm 19:7-11_____

_____

Psalm 33:4 _____

Psalm 119:89 _____

Psalm 119:105 _____

Psalm 119:130 _____

Psalm 119:138 _____

Psalm 119:160 _____

Proverbs 30:5 _____

Isaiah 40:8 _____

I like to use several different versions of the Bible when I'm looking up verses. Here are some of the words and phrases used to described God's Word that I found the most meaningful out of these passages: "righteous altogether", "settled in heaven", "tested" (NASB); "radiant and giving light" (NIV); "very essence of your words is truth", "proves true" (NLT); "every GOD-direction is road-tested", "solid to the core", "revelation is whole and pulls our lives together . . . accurate down to the nth degree", "right on target", "all add up to the sum total—truth", "stands firm and forever" (MSG).

Only God's Word will stand forever. I've read many outstanding books that have had a profound effect on my life. But, the truth is this: everything written by man will fade away. Typically within a generation of the writing of a book (or less!), its audience and ability to influence will be lost and it will be replaced with a new book, a new author, a new approach. That's what's so important about making God's Word a priority: it will never grow old or become useless. It is applicable to every generation because it is God's complete written revelation of truth—eternal and unchanging.

Psalm 119:105 even tells us that God's Word lights up our path through the false "truths", values, and philosophies of this world and reveals all of their roots that could entangle us. Like using a flashlight to walk through the woods at night, we can count on God's Word to keep us from groping around in the darkness. Since God is reliable and unchangeable and embodies perfect truth, we can expect his Word to be dependable and true rather than devious or erratic. As we see in creation, when God speaks, there is order and goodness instead of chaos. But, as Psalm 119:160 reminds us, we must take *all* of God's words together in order to find truth. We cannot place our faith in portions of the Bible without believing all of what it says.

When we turn to the New Testament, we find the importance of this stressed again and the practical side of God's Word discussed in two major passages. Read each of them and write what they have to say about God's Word:

2 Timothy 3:16-17 _____

_____

_____

Hebrews 4:12 _____

_____

Did you find words like these to describe the Bible: "God-breathed" (NIV); "profitable, adequate" (NASB); "proficient, well-fitted, alive, full of power, active, operative, energizing, effective" (AMP)? Did you discover that the Bible acts in these ways: to "teach, prepare, equip, correct", "exposes innermost thoughts and desires" (NLT); "judges . . . intentions" (NASB); "judges thoughts and attitudes" (NIV); "sifting, analyzing" (AMP); "exposing our rebellion" (MSG)?

These passages help us to recognize that the Bible is not a human book and is not simply a collection of words from God. As 2 Peter 1:20-21 tells us, Scripture reveals God's person and plan; and it is completely trustworthy because God was in control of the whole process as it was written. Because God was actively involved, the Bible is infallible. God was the source of its content, and what it says is what God has said; and, as Hebrews 4:12 shows us, the Bible is living, dynamic, and life-changing.

What this means for us is that God's Word is entirely authoritative for our life of faith. It is our standard for testing everything else, our safeguard against false teaching, and our source of guidance. The Bible penetrates a person's innermost being, revealing who we are and what we are not, cutting through to the core of our moral and spiritual life.

I experienced the reality of this once as a young teenage Christian. I had just participated in something that I knew was wrong in God's eyes but that I had chosen to do anyway. There were no serious long-term ramifications, and there was little chance for anyone besides me to find out what I'd done. But God knew; and, as I felt convicted by his Spirit, this is the portion of God's Word that my eyes fell upon: "Nothing in all creation is hidden from God's sight. Everything is uncovered and laid bare before the eyes of him to whom we must give account" (Hebrews 4:13, NIV). It wasn't news to me that God saw everything I did; but these words of God at that moment in time and at that age had a profound and lasting effect upon my life. Living and active indeed.

It is important to remember that the knowledge and truth we discover in the Bible is active in accomplishing God's purposes and requires us to make decisions. Knowledge alone is not useful (as with my first religion professor) unless it strengthens our faith and leads us to do God's work in the world.

In Isaiah 55:10-11, God tells us that his words never return empty without achieving the purpose that he wants. The *New Living Translation* says God's Word "always produces fruit", and another version says it like this: " . . . not come back empty-handed . . . will complete the assignment" (MSG). We humans speak so many worthless and meaningless words. Isn't it encouraging to know that absolutely everything God ever says, from before time began and for all of eternity (and everything in between), has meaning, purpose, and success built into it? Those are the types of words I can rest my very life on and trust to guide and sustain me.

Another important thing to remember as we approach God's Word is to recognize the role of the Bible in the "big picture". God first expressed himself in creation and history; then God sent Jesus to help us see how he thinks (see John 1:14-17). As John 3:33-34 tells us, Jesus certified that God is truthful; and other passages tell us that Jesus is the truth that sets us free (John 14:6 and 8:31-36). Jesus is the reality of all of God's promises throughout history. But the Bible that we have today is the completed Word of God—the final expression of his thought, will, and action. We have been given the Holy Spirit, whose very essence and action is truth (see John 14:15-17, 15:15, and 16:13-15), to help us as we study God's Word.

Notice in the John 16 passage that all three members of the trinity—Father, Son, and Spirit—are tied together and unified by truth. We can trust the Bible to be truth from God because of the life Jesus lived and the work of the Spirit in our hearts. Each validates the other and leads us to the complete Word of God that can direct every part of our lives.

Most Christians would agree that trusting God's Word is the first step in living the life of faith; but what does that look like on a practical level? How does believing what God has said in Scripture make a difference in our everyday lives? In a culture that bombards us daily with immeasurable amounts of stimuli and innumerable choices, how do we make God's Word our primary choice that affects all other decisions? How do we reach the point where God's Word, and precious little else, guides our path through life?

I have been a Christian for forty-eight years, coming to a place of "saving faith" as a young child. For most of the first nearly forty years of my Christian walk, I was a growing follower who sought God and his will and way in all of life's circumstances. I read and studied the Bible alone and with others on a regular basis, and I faced life's challenges with a strong and unwavering faith and a desire to please God with my life and grow closer to him no matter what. I was a "good Christian", and my walk usually matched my talk. During this time I went to college, married, raised two children, and served in numerous ministries and positions of leadership at church. Though not without my share of major difficult circumstances, I had a good and fulfilling life and usually felt I was "making a difference". I based my entire life on God's Word and revered it as my guide.

Then almost everything changed. In the course of about four years (and mostly within the time span of a few months), every aspect of my life except my marriage took on a new look. God was leading me into a different and difficult chapter of my life. Here are the facts:

After serving in ministry in the same church for all of my adult life, I felt God leading me to leave my twenty-five-year commitment to worship ministry and wait on him for the next step. As I later discovered, I would wait nearly five years. Part of this waiting on God included the very difficult process of leaving the church body I had been a member of for thirty-eight years and finding a new church home. This decision was met with every response from misunderstanding to outright rejection and resulted in strained relationships with my extended family and the eventual loss of most friendships from this previous body of believers. During this same time period, I suffered a cardiac event requiring surgery and a complete lifestyle change; and my husband and I experienced the failure of our business, months of unemployment, and the eventual necessity of filing bankruptcy (due to debt from the business) and being forced to sell our home to avoid a foreclosure sale, a home which had been personally designed for my parents by my architect brother and was a substantial investment for my entire extended family. After living in the same town for twenty-one years, we moved to a new one. I began working outside the home after nearly twenty-four years of being a fulltime homemaker, and my husband started a new job in a completely different career field. I faced the effects of serious sin and Satan's schemes in one of my children and experienced the process of both of my sons leaving home to attend college and eventually for good. And my father, my mother's only faithful companion for over fifty-six years, was diagnosed with leukemia and went to be with the Lord after a four-year battle.

Those are the facts, but the effects were even more life-changing. For the first time in my life, I experienced a complete loss of hope and a real lack of purpose. While I continued to seek God and knew he was the answer, I had difficulty finding him. I will elaborate more on this in a later chapter, but the important result was this: I eventually moved from my previous reverence for God's Word and my trust in God's truth to a new love for the Bible and a passion to help others discover the same. Through the writings of other Christian authors and the direction of God's Spirit in the process, certain portions of Scripture became key verses that changed the downward spiral of my emotions. The words of God in the Bible began to speak directly to me on a regular basis; and, as I searched the pages of Scripture for words that ministered to me where I was at and how I felt, I found the Bible to be alive, active, and relevant in a way I had never experienced before. After so many years of faithfully following God, I learned to love and desire his Word in a new way. I also learned the power of praying God's Word—for myself and for my loved ones. I discovered that what I used to think was boring and contrived became not only the best words I could pray, but sometimes the *only* words I could come up with (special thanks to Beth Moore here[2]). While I always believed in the power of God's Word to change lives, I experienced this transformation firsthand in a powerful and truly liberating way. Ancient words now became *my* words for living today. In the pages ahead, I will share many of "my verses" and tell you how God used his Word to speak directly in various situations. For now, let me just share the one all-encompassing verse that became my own as I walked through this time without hope or purpose, Romans 15:13: " . . . God, *the source of hope*, will fill you completely with *joy* and *peace* because you *trust* in him. Then you will *overflow* with *confident hope* through the power of the Holy Spirit." (NLT, emphasis mine). God showed me that the only thing *I* had to do was trust; *hope, joy* and *peace* were God's responsibility and gracious gifts to me.

So does everyone have to experience such difficult life changes to know the power of God's Word and learn to trust his words for every part of life? Probably not. God works uniquely in each person, and no two lives will be transformed in the same way. But Christian history does seem to show us that those who have experienced deeper difficulties also often experience a deeper transformation in ways that would not be possible without the difficulties. This should encourage us to be more willing to *enter in* and *embrace* difficult times and to turn to God's Word for the answers we need in those moments. My prayer for you is that you will seek God until he finds you and learn the importance of basing your very life on what he says to you, trusting his Word implicitly and desiring it more than anything this world can offer. It alone is eternal and worth our time and effort; everything else, even other "good" things, will pass away. Let God's Word transform the rest of your life on earth and the life you will live for eternity.

Why is what we believe *about* the Bible just as important as our knowledge of what it says? _____

_____

_____

What things besides God's Word do people put their faith in and rely on for living? _____

_____

_____

What things besides God's Word, maybe even "good" things, have *you* relied on in the past or even now? _____

_____

_____

Out of all the passages we looked up previously in this chapter, which description of God's Word is the most meaningful to you, and why?

_____

_____

_____

What are the three ways that God has revealed himself to us since the beginning of time? _____

_____

_____

Read John 16:13-15. What is the one thing that unifies the three members of the trinity and validates the work they do? _____

_____

Think about all of the options available to us living in the twenty-first century. Why is it important to have absolute truth to believe in? _____

_____

_____

_____

Look up Romans 15:13, Psalm 119:165, and 1 Peter 1:22-23. What results of trusting God's Word are described in these verses? _____

_____

_____

_____

What results have *you* experienced so far since you began trusting God's Word? _____

_____

_____

Lesson 3

Trusting God's Sovereignty

Once we decide that God's Word is going to be our source for truth and what we place our trust in, we are able to move from basic knowledge about and belief in God to specific God–attributes to believe in. The first attribute that we discover resoundingly in the Bible is God's sovereignty, which isn't so much an *attribute* as a *prerogative* based on who he is. But we immediately encounter a problem: our finite minds are incapable of fully comprehending an infinite God. Our severely limited understanding immediately affects our perception of God. And our limited vocabulary and terminology, which is all we have to work with, inadvertently affects our ability to describe God fully. Because our own human experience is inherently limited, we sometimes get confused about who God really is in relation to all we experience. We have a narrow view of God instead of a Biblical view of God. Therefore, we need to look directly at God's Word in order to try as best we can to comprehend what it means for God to be sovereign, to have "no external restraint", to have "dominion over all forms of existence".[1]

We encounter the sovereignty of God from the first book of the Bible to the very last. God is both the beginning and the end, the supreme ruler of past, present, and future. In Revelation 1:4-5, he is "the one who is, who always was, and who is still to come"

(NLT); and in verse 8 he is "the Alpha and the Omega" (NLT), which are the first and last letters of the Greek alphabet—the "A to Z" (MSG). In Genesis 1:1, we see that God is distinct from all creation and created by no one. He has always been, eternal and in control; and all reality as we know it is "God-shaped and God-filled".[2] Eugene Peterson, the author of *The Message* translation of the Bible, says it this way: "First, God. God is the subject of life. God is foundational for living. If we don't have a sense of the primacy of God, we will never get it right, get life right, get *our* lives right. Not God at the margins; not God as an option; not God on the weekends. God at center and circumference; God first and last; God, God, God . . . God is the commanding and accompanying presence that provides both plot and texture to every sentence"[3] of our story. It seems that it is of primary importance for a life of faith that we understand to the best of our ability what is involved in God's sovereignty.

Look up the following verses and list the different ways that God's sovereignty is described. (It would be helpful to use more than one version of the Bible if you have that available to you.)

1 Chronicles 29:11-12 _____

_____

Psalm 47:5-8 _____

_____

Psalm 50:1 _____

_____

Psalm 66:7 _____

_____

Psalm 75:3 & 7 _____

_____

Psalm 93:1-2 _____

_____

Psalm 115:3 _____

_____

Psalm 135:6 _____

Isaiah 40:15 & 17 _____

Isaiah 45:18 _____

Hebrews 4:13 _____

Revelation 11:17 _____

Let me share my favorites of the images painted in these verses from the translations I use: God is "Lord over earth . . . King of the mountain" (MSG), he "summons the earth" (NIV), and he says "it is I who hold its pillars firm" (NIV). In the world that the Psalms were written (the ancient Near East), the word "pillars" was a reference to the part of a temple that gave it stability. So Psalm 75:3 tells us that, regardless of the crumbling state of the world's moral order, God is the one who stabilizes everything and in fact guarantees stability. We are also told that he "picks up the whole earth" (NLT). He is able to do this because his throne "has stood from time immemorial", and he is "from the everlasting past" (NLT). This is helpful to remember when we read that God is "doing whatever he wants to do", that he "does just as he pleases—however, wherever, whenever", or that "the nations add up to simply nothing . . . less than nothing is more like it. A minus" (MSG).

The obvious implication from these verses is this: God is always present even when we are unaware of him. God has unlimited power and control of all of the world's events, which is in sharp contrast to our very limited perspective of just about everything. We simply cannot see all that God is doing or all that God *will* do. And, while these few verses from the Bible are certainly not exhaustive on the topic of God's sovereignty, they help us begin to get the picture of how different God is from us and what it means to trust in such a big God.

As we first discovered in Lesson 2, each member of the trinity is involved in who God is. In terms of God's sovereignty, we now discover the way that Jesus fully embodied this characteristic of God and how his resurrection took it to a new level, providing us with a new way of understanding what God's sovereignty looks like. The most complete and expressive Scripture passage on this is Colossians 1:15-20:

> "He is the image of the invisible God, the firstborn over all creation. For by him all things were created: things in heaven and on earth, visible and invisible, whether thrones or powers or rulers or authorities; all things were created by him and for him. He is before all things, and in him all things hold together. And he is the head of the body, the church; he is the beginning and the firstborn from among the dead, so that in everything he might have the supremacy. For God was pleased to have all his fullness dwell in him, and through him to reconcile to himself all things, whether things on earth or things in heaven, by making peace through his blood, shed on the cross." (NIV)

It is clear from these verses that Jesus is Lord of all and that he has no equal or rival. Christ is all of God in human form, which means he has priority, preeminence, and authority over all creation. And his resurrection proves that he is also spiritually supreme. When the apostle Paul wrote to the Colossian church, he used the word "fullness" in verse 19 because it was a term his readers would have been very familiar with. As part of the vocabulary of the Greek philosophy of Gnosticism, "fullness" referred to the sum of the supernatural forces controlling people's fate. So Paul was making sure that all of his readers (which includes us!) understood that Jesus Christ, though fully human, was also *fully* divine, including God's undisputed Old Testament characteristic of sovereignty.

Now that we have looked at an overview of what the Bible teaches about God's sovereignty, let's get more specific. There are numerous stories from the Old Testament which support the truth that God is sovereign, including Noah and the flood, Joseph and his brothers, Moses and the exodus, the fall of Jericho, Naomi and Ruth, David and Goliath, Elijah, Elisha, Esther, Daniel and the lions' den, and Jonah. For the Hebrew people, the sovereignty of God was never in dispute. But perhaps the most familiar story lasts for an entire book of the Old Testament: the story of Job. And, while Job's story is often referred to in terms of suffering and a discussion on God's role and action in our suffering, I want to approach the story of Job as an amazing example of God's sovereignty and see what we can learn from individual passages in this story that will impact our story as well. The actual plot is laid out for us in the first two chapters, with the rest of the book revealing various responses to the plot: Job's, his three friends', an interested bystander's, and finally God's. After being told some background material on who Job was, we are given the basic story in Job 1:6-2:10:

> "One day the members of the heavenly court came to present themselves before the LORD, and the Accuser, Satan, came with them. 'Where have you come from?' the LORD asked Satan. Satan answered the LORD, 'I have been patrolling the earth, watching everything that's going on.' Then the LORD asked Satan, 'Have you noticed my servant Job? He is the finest man in all the earth. He is blameless—a man of complete integrity. He fears God and stays away from evil.' Satan replied to the LORD, 'Yes, but Job has good reason to fear God. You have always put a wall of protection around him and his homes and his

property. You have made him prosper in everything he does. Look how rich he is! But reach out and take away everything he has, and he will surely curse you to your face!' 'All right, you may test him,' the LORD said to Satan. 'Do whatever you want with everything he possesses, but don't harm him physically.' So Satan left the LORD's presence.

One day when Job's sons and daughters were feasting at the oldest brother's house, a messenger arrived at Job's home with this news: 'Your oxen were plowing, with the donkeys feeding beside them, when the Sabeans raided us. They stole all the animals and killed all the farmhands. I am the only one who escaped to tell you.' While he was still speaking, another messenger arrived with this news: 'The fire of God has fallen from heaven and burned up your sheep and all the shepherds. I am the only one who escaped to tell you.' While he was still speaking, a third messenger arrived with this news: 'Three bands of Chaldean raiders have stolen your camels and killed your servants. I am the only one who escaped to tell you.' While he was still speaking, another messenger arrived with this news: 'Your sons and daughters were feasting in their oldest brother's home. Suddenly, a powerful wind swept in from the wilderness and hit the house on all sides. The house collapsed, and all your children are dead. I am the only one who escaped to tell you.'

Job stood up and tore his robe in grief. Then he shaved his head and fell to the ground to worship. He said, 'I came naked from my mother's womb, and I will be naked when I leave. The LORD gave me what I had, and the LORD has taken it away. Praise the name of the LORD!' In all of this, Job did not sin by blaming God.

One day the members of the heavenly court came again to present themselves before the LORD, and the Accuser, Satan, came with them. 'Where have you come from?' the LORD asked Satan. Satan answered the LORD, 'I have been patrolling the earth, watching everything that's going on.' Then the LORD asked Satan, 'Have you noticed my servant Job? He is the finest man in all the earth. He is blameless—a man of complete integrity. He fears God and stays away from evil. And he has maintained his integrity, even though you urged me to harm him without cause.' Satan replied to the LORD, 'Skin for skin! A man will give up everything he has to save his life. But reach out and take away his health, and he will surely curse you to your face!' 'All right, do with him as you please,' the LORD said to Satan. 'But spare his life.' So Satan left the LORD's presence, and he struck Job with terrible boils from head to foot.

Job scraped his skin with a piece of broken pottery as he sat among the ashes. His wife said to him, 'Are you still trying to maintain your integrity? Curse God and die.' But Job replied, 'You talk like a foolish woman. Should we accept only good things from the hand of God and never anything bad?' So in all this, Job said nothing wrong." (NLT)

So what do these verses tell us about God's sovereignty? To start with, we see that God controls the whole story. All of the angels are compelled to present themselves before God (see 1:6 and 2:1), and this includes Satan. It is God who asks the questions and demands answers. Satan thinks he's in control, but he's not. Secondly, in verse 12 of chapter 1 and in 2:6, we see that Satan is kept on a leash. He is limited by God's power and can only do what he is permitted to do. And, lastly, we see not only that God cannot be stirred up to do things against his will, but also that he is fully aware of every attempt by Satan to bring suffering and difficulty upon Job and us. God cannot be fooled by Satan: God is in control of the world, and only he understands why good people like Job are allowed to suffer. Job's suffering was a test for Job, Satan, and us—not for God. Everything that happens is part of his divine purpose even if we don't understand it. Trusting God's sovereignty cannot be separated from an understanding and trust of his other character traits: love, mercy, compassion, grace, wisdom, and justice.

We'll talk more about that in a minute, but let's finish looking at the story of Job. Beginning in chapter 3, we have thirty-five chapters of conversations between Job, his friends, and a bystander as they try to make sense of what God has allowed in his life. As you can imagine, in that amount of time and words they pretty much exhaust the realm of speculation on *why* God allowed such intense suffering in Job's life! But here's something I notice: in all those words, the sovereignty of God is never questioned. Many other traits of God are talked about, but God's sovereignty is taken for granted. While Job and his peers don't understand why everything happened the way it did, they accept without argument that God was in control. And, in the process of discussion, they provide us with some wonderful passages of Scripture that help us to describe God's sovereignty better and also help us to begin to form our response to that sovereignty. Look at these three passages in particular:

> "He spreads the skies over unformed space, hangs the earth out in empty space. He pours water into cumulus cloud-bags and the bags don't burst. He makes the moon wax and wane, putting it through its phases. He draws the horizon out over the ocean, sets a boundary between light and darkness. Thunder crashes and rumbles in the skies. Listen! It's God raising his voice! By his power he stills sea storms, by his wisdom he tames sea monsters. With one breath he clears the sky, with one finger he crushes the sea serpent. And this is only the beginning, a mere whisper

of his rule. Whatever would we do if he really raised his voice!" Job 26:7-14, MSG

"God alone understands the way to wisdom; he knows where it can be found, for he looks throughout the whole earth and sees everything under the heavens. He decided how hard the winds should blow and how much rain should fall. He made the laws for the rain and laid out a path for the lightning. Then he saw wisdom and evaluated it. He set it in place and examined it thoroughly." Job 28:23-27, NLT

"How great is God—beyond our understanding! The number of his years is past finding out. He draws up the drops of water, which distill as rain to the streams; the clouds pour down their moisture and abundant showers fall on mankind. Who can understand how he spreads out the clouds, how he thunders from his pavilion? See how he scatters his lightning about him, bathing the depths of the sea." Job 36:26-30, NIV

In Job 26, we see that what God has revealed to us about his rule over natural and supernatural forces amounts to no more than a whisper. If it is difficult for us to comprehend the little that we know about God, how much more impossible it would be for us to understand the full extent of his power! In the Job 28 passage, we see that God is the author of all wisdom and the only one who really understands it. In fact, what we humans call "wisdom" is not even true wisdom, which Job 28:28 and Proverbs 1:7 reveal as "the fear of the Lord". And, in chapter 36, a young man named Elihu continues these themes by reminding Job and us that God is incomprehensible: we cannot know him completely. We can never know enough to answer all of life's questions, to predict our own future, or to manipulate God for our own ends. These verses are a good start for us, but then God speaks.

Read Job 38:4–39:30 and 40:15–41:34, then answer the following questions:

List several descriptions or phrases from 38:4–38 that God uses to show Job and us that all of inanimate creation testifies to his sovereignty and power. _____

_____

_____

_____

What specific actions are under God's control rather than ours? ___

_____

_____

_____

From 38:39–39:30, 40:15, and 41:1, name several animals that God uses as examples of his sovereignty over creatures. _____

_____

_____

_____

List five specific actions that God does for animals that they cannot do for themselves (see 38:39, 38:41, 39:5, 39:19, 39:26–27). _____

_____

_____

_____

Here are my favorite word pictures that God uses to illustrate his sovereignty: "laid the foundations of the earth . . . determined its dimensions . . . stretched out the surveying line" (NLT); "came up with the blueprints and measurements . . . set the cornerstone" (MSG); "enclosed the sea with doors" (NASB); "limited its shores" (NLT); "made a playpen for it" (MSG); "commanded the morning . . . caused the dawn to know its place" (NASB); "know where the gates of death are located" (NLT); "carves canyons for . . . rain, and charts the route of thunderstorms . . . the father of rain and dew, the

mother of ice and frost" (MSG); "know the laws of the heavens . . .
set up (God's) dominion over the earth" (NIV); "gives intuition to
the heart and instinct to the mind" (NLT); "prepares for the raven
its nourishment" (NASB); "through your know-how . . . the hawk
learned to fly . . . you command the eagle's flight, and teach her to
build her nest in the heights" (MSG).

What do we learn about God's sovereignty from all of these words
and God's lengthy response to Job? What is the point that will make
a difference for us? God seems to sum it up in Job 41:11: "*Whatever
is under the whole heaven is Mine*" (NASB), or "I'm in *charge* of all
this—I *run* this universe!" (MSG). The point of all of God's rhetorical
questions to Job was to get him to recognize and submit to divine
power and sovereignty so he could hear what God was *really* saying
to him. God demonstrated his love and care for Job by coming to
him, which a sovereign God didn't have to do; but he didn't answer
Job's questions (or ours) about suffering and justice because these
were (are) not at the heart of the issue. God simply showed Job and
us that there is no standard or criterion higher than himself by which
to judge what we see and experience. God himself is the standard,
and our only option is to submit to his authority and rest in his care.
Getting all the answers is not the point; trusting without answers
is. God's response succeeds in bringing Job (and hopefully us) to
complete faith in God's goodness *without* receiving direct answers
to the problems at hand. Which is, of course, the point of faith and
trust. The sovereignty of God is a place we can rest in spite of what
life brings and regardless of our inability to know the reasons behind
our circumstances.

Look at Job's response to God's sovereignty: "I am nothing—how could
I ever find the answers? I will cover my mouth with my hand. I have said
too much already. I have nothing more to say" (Job 40:3-5, NLT). The
New International Version translates the first phrase as "unworthy", and
the Hebrew word for this can also mean "small" or "insignificant".
Another famous Biblical person's response to God's sovereignty is
found in Isaiah 6:1-5. When confronted with a vision of God and

heaven, Isaiah says, "It's all over! I am doomed, for I am a sinful man" (NLT). These responses represent a healthy respect for who God is in light of who we are not. But, beyond shrinking back in awe of God, we need to reach a point where God's sovereignty becomes personal to us and where we can live our lives in *confidence* instead of *fear* because God is sovereign. Certainly, worship is a natural and necessary response; and there are some wonderful contemporary songs that help us in this process. Not long ago I found this one by Shannon J. Wexelberg, which states it well:

> "I am overcome by your goodness
> I am overwhelmed by your lovingkindness
> I am swept away by your mercy
> And I am lifting my hands to the One who fills me.
> I am so amazed at your greatness
> So in awe of what You have done to save us
> I am bowing down to your holiness, my Lord
> I am undone."[4]

Worship is an important place to start, but it doesn't complete the picture of how we trust God's sovereignty. Recently, I spent a year reading *The One Year Book of Christian History*, a devotional book with daily readings about all kinds of Christians who have lived from the time of Christ until the present. It is subtitled *A Daily Glimpse Into God's Powerful Work* and is intended to be a book of encouragement for each of us in our walk with God based on what he has done in the past in others' lives.[5] Unfortunately, I was reading this book during one of the most difficult years of my life—a year when I was struggling with God's sovereignty on a regular basis. While I was encouraged at times during the year, more often than not I found myself depressed by some of the horrible things God had allowed to happen to some of his greatest saints. Because of my own "present sufferings" (Romans 8:18, NIV), I found it difficult to trust God's sovereignty and truly believe what Romans 8:28 goes on to say: "And we know that God causes everything to work together for the good of those who love God and are called according to his purpose for them" (NLT).

It's much easier to read about someone like Job or past saints than it is for us to turn what we read into something personal that changes *our* relationship with God. When God's sovereignty and our circumstances collide, we often struggle to have the right response. But what *is* the right response? If we focus too heavily on the "I'm God and you're not" side, we can become fatalistic, believing that nothing we do or say really matters in God's scheme of things; and, if we focus too heavily on the "Woe is me" side, we simply become depressed. A healthy balance includes a broader knowledge of *all* of God's characteristics combined, which allows our circumstances to be understood in relation to all of who God is and not just his sovereignty. Notice how well the song quoted above combines many of God's characteristics: while using such knee-bowing responses to sovereignty as "overcome, overwhelmed, swept away, amazed, in awe, and undone", Wexelberg reminds us of some of God's other characteristics that work together with his sovereignty—goodness, lovingkindness, mercy, greatness, holiness, and his actions of saving and filling us. His sovereignty provides the framework for his other characteristics to be exercised in full measure and in conjunction with the reality of our power of moral choice. To avoid blaming him for everything bad that happens or viewing him as an uncaring controller, it is essential that we see God in his entirety. Because there is a sovereign someone behind every part of the world's order and function, we have a place where we fit and have a purpose; and, because this sovereign someone has allowed us to have free choice, we are not merely pawns.

An important part of learning to trust God's sovereignty is understanding that it has a personal side directed toward me. What Eugene Peterson has to say is a good reminder: "God is sovereign. God rules. Not only in our personal affairs, but in the cosmos. Not only in our times and places of worship, but in office buildings, political affairs, factories, universities, hospitals—yes, even behind the scenes in saloons and rock concerts . . . Yet not much in our daily experience confirms it. Impersonal forces and arrogant egos compete for the last word in power. Most of us are knocked around much of the time by forces and wills that give no hint of God." We must remember that "every day we wake up in the middle of something that is already going on, that has been going on for a long time: geneology and geology, history and culture, the cosmos—God. We are neither accidental nor incidental to the story."[6] Believing that God's sovereignty includes a *personal* interest in me and a commitment to my *good* makes all the difference in my ability to trust when life feels bad and impersonal.

It means that, when my son Brad was put in the hospital at the age of three with a possible diagnosis of leukemia or meningitis, I could entrust him to God's care and tell God I would still follow his leading even if he chose to take Brad from this world (despite the fact that a time of infertility meant I had waited over two years for his arrival and that he held a special place in my heart). It means that, when I was diagnosed with lymphoma as a young mother of a nine-year-old and a four-year-old, I could trust God to take care of my children if he chose not to heal me. It means that, when my husband and I struggled for several months to keep our business afloat and eventually experienced the humiliation and financial ramifications of closing it down, we could trust that God was not surprised or indifferent and that he had a purpose beyond what we could see. And it means that God is watching whenever we endure abusive or ungodly treatment from others, even fellow Christians or God-ordained leaders, and that we can trust God to have the final say and use every good and bad thing we humans do to somehow bring glory to himself. (As mentioned earlier, you can see that none of God's characteristics stands alone: they are all intertwined. We will discuss many more of these characteristics in later chapters; so, if you're currently struggling with trusting God's sovereignty, don't give up! Hopefully these later lessons will be helpful to you.)

During college, my son usually attended an annual Christian music festival put on by his college which he looked forward to with great anticipation. One year, he called me shortly before the two-day festival began, and I was struck by how excited and anxious he was to be in the presence of many of his favorite bands. He always arrived early and made every effort to be in the very front near the stage. At the end of the second day, he had no voice left and proudly announced that he had been on his feet for the past twelve hours straight, not to mention the day before! As I thought about our response to *daily* being in the presence of a sovereign God, I couldn't help but see the contrast. Most of the world doesn't really care about being in God's presence, and many Christians just don't "get it". Or we understand in small doses, perhaps in an especially inspiring worship service on Sunday morning, but not all the time. I think we prove that we "get it" by *trusting* God's sovereignty on a daily basis and by remembering what Peter tells us in 1 Peter 1:17: " . . . live your lives as strangers here in reverent fear" (NIV). As the *New Living Translation* puts it, Christians are "foreigners in the land". This world is not our home; we are citizens of heaven (see Philippians 3:20). What we experience here on earth is not supposed to make sense or feel "right" because we are not living in the world we were created for. Trusting God's sovereignty proves that we understand this truth and ensures that we are living as God intends us to as long as we are here on earth.

Name one life experience you have had where God's sovereignty and your circumstances have "collided". _____

_____

Have you typically found it easy or hard to trust God's sovereignty? Why do you think this is so? _____

_____

_____

_____

What other characteristics of God do you find helpful in balancing your view of God's sovereignty? _____

_____

_____

How does it help you trust God's sovereignty to know that he has a *personal* interest in you and is committed to your *good*? _____

_____

_____

_____

What does it mean to live as a stranger in this world, and how does that perspective help you to trust God's sovereignty? _____

_____

_____

_____

Lesson 4

Trusting God's Thoughts Toward You

Learning about God's sovereignty helps us to recognize God's place in relation to the whole world and our place in relation to God, but it doesn't tell me a lot about what he thinks about me *personally*. As humans, we live in a relational world where what we think about others and what others think about us makes a difference in our relationships. If I'm going to have a personal relationship of faith with a sovereign God, I have to move beyond his sovereignty and learn to trust the thoughts that he directs toward *me* and not just toward the world in general. But, precisely because we're human, we immediately run into problems because, as Isaiah 55:8-9 reminds us, our thoughts and God's thoughts are nothing alike.

We have all met people that appear arrogant, self-absorbed, or to think a lot of themselves. We find ourselves being frustrated with them while at the same time wishing we could feel better about ourselves like they do. The truth of the matter is that most humans at one time or another (or maybe most of the time?) feel unworthy, insignificant, ordinary—and struggle with low self-esteem, depression, or both. Adding to this common secular scenario is the Christian emphasis on humility and traits like meekness and gentleness. Human beings rarely if ever achieve balance in anything: we are usually somewhere in the process of moving from one extreme of the pendulum swing to the other. So, as Christians, we tend to turn humility and meekness into unworthiness and self-esteem issues; or, in our effort to feel better about ourselves, we "perform" for God and come across as arrogant or prideful. We lose track of Paul's words to us in Romans 12:3: "The only accurate way to understand ourselves is by what God is and by what he does for us, not by what we are and what we do for him" (MSG). "True humility is not convincing yourself that you are worthless but recognizing God's work in you. It is having God's perspective on who you are . . ."[1]

To compound the situation, all of us are affected by our past and the thoughts of others toward us, whether spoken or unspoken. In varying degrees based on our individual personalities, we all want to be thought well of. We all want to "fit in" with someone; and, even if we don't often seek the favor of men in a secular sense, we don't want to be left out of *everything*. We all need to know that *someone* really cares about us and thinks good things about us. And yet our experiences include such things as unloving and harsh parents, physical, emotional, or sexual abuse, exclusion or rejection by others, unkind words and actions directed at us (even by fellow Christians), and our own myriad of personal and relationship failures. We are imperfect humans who live in an imperfect world, and Satan is alive and well. It seems almost impossible to "be honest in your evaluation of yourselves" (Rom. 12:3, NLT) and learn to trust God's thoughts toward us and function daily based on *his* thoughts and not all the rest. But this is what we are called to do.

Once again we find that, if we are going to trust God, we cannot accomplish it by looking at our daily lives and circumstances. It is imperative that we look at God's Word to find out what God's thoughts toward us are so that we can focus on those thoughts and effectively overcome the enemy's assaults on our own thoughts. The Bible gives us a lot of information about God's thoughts toward us, so this shouldn't be too difficult. Let's start by looking at the very first interaction between God and man, in Genesis 1:26-27:

"God spoke: 'Let us make human beings in our image, make them reflecting our nature, so they can be responsible for the fish in the sea, the birds in the air, the cattle, and yes, Earth itself, and every animal that moves on the face of Earth.' God created human beings; he created them godlike, reflecting God's nature, He created them male and female." (MSG)

What words in this passage tell us that God thinks differently about humans than the other things he created? _____

_____

_____

Now read these verses and answer the questions that follow:

Psalm 8:3-5—What position do humans have in God's creation and what have we been given? _____

_____

_____

Psalm 139:13-17—What kinds of thoughts are we told that God has toward us? _____

_____

_____

To know that we are made in the image of God should provide us with a solid basis for self-worth regardless of what others think about us. The words "image" and "likeness" are synonyms and include all of God's characteristics. *The Message* translation of Genesis 1:26 quoted above says that humans reflect God's nature, which means that God's character goes into the creation of every person. Therefore, each of us is worthy of honor and respect because we bear the stamp of the Creator. The Hebrew words used in Psalm 139:13 indicate that God knows our "innermost center of emotions and moral sensitivity"[2]—the place where most of us fail regularly.

God knows us perfectly, inside and out, and yet considers us highly valuable, creating us only a little lower than himself and the angels. Because God has already declared us valuable, we should have as much respect for ourselves as he does and be set free from feelings of worthlessness. God has bestowed high dignity on humans, and to question our worth is to question God's work. We already have God's approval, and we need to constantly remind ourselves that we really only live our lives for an audience of One.

When we discussed God's sovereignty, we discovered that God is the ruler of everything and that he is the controlling force behind everything. From our human understanding and experience with *human* rulers, we might be led to believe that God is too busy ruling and controlling to think any specific thoughts about any portion of his creation. But the following verses remind us that God is capable of doing both: looking at the big picture while at the same time caring about specific details.

What specific God-thoughts or actions does each of these verses reveal (try using different translations of the Bible)?

Psalm 8:4 _____

_____

Psalm 40:1 _____

_____

Jeremiah 29:12 _____

_____

We see that God turns to us, listens to us, thinks about us, is "mindful" of us (Hebrews 2:6, NIV, a New Testament quote of Psalm 8:4). These are all *personal* thoughts and actions and go beyond the "big picture" concept of sovereignty. The word "mindful" literally means to remember; and, in the Bible, "remember" is not just to recall, but also to express concern for or to act with loving care for. *The Amplified New Testament* translates Hebrews 2:6 like this: "What is man that

You are mindful of him . . . that You graciously *and* helpfully care for *and* visit *and* look after him?" I like the idea conveyed in one translation of Psalm 40:1: "He *inclined* to me . . ." (NASB, emphasis mine). God is not only paying attention to us, but he is also choosing to be involved with the details of our lives and "incline" toward us. At least in my experience, this is something that humans tend to fail miserably at; so I am grateful that I don't have to wonder whether God will respond in the same way.

But actually *trusting* these God-thoughts toward me requires a better understanding of the character traits of God that motivate his thoughts and actions toward me: his love, his patience, and his goodness. These are the attributes of God that provide a framework for his thoughts and actions toward us; and, since they are attributes that are totally foreign to us as humans (apart from God), we need some help in this area.

First of all, let's look at God's love. The phrase "God is love" has become cliché in our twenty-first century culture. To say that God is love tends to raise more questions than provide answers or encouragement for us; but most of the reason for this is that we have lost track of what love really is. Eugene Peterson, in his preface to the book of Hosea (an unlikely love story) in *The Message* translation of the Bible, puts it this way: "The huge, mountainous reality of all existence is that God is love, that God loves the world. Each single detail of the real world that we face and deal with day after day is permeated by this love . . . God loves us . . . goes after us at our worst, keeps after us until he gets us, and makes lovers of men and women who know nothing of real love."[3] In order to understand what real love—God's love—is, we need to look beyond our cultural lies and influences and back to the source of all truth: God's Word. In Psalm 119:76, we see that God's "unfailing love" (NIV) is intended to comfort us. Another translation is "lovingkindness" (NASB), and the Hebrew word for this denotes befriending. At the very least, God is our friend and his love is kind and will always be there. But this is just a start.

The classic Biblical passage on love is 1 Corinthians 13:4–8a, which is often used at Christian weddings to describe our goal in marriage. Rightly so, but all of us find out soon after marriage (if not before!) that this kind of love is unattainable by humans. That is because primarily this passage is a description of *perfect* love: the love that God has for us and models for us perfectly. So, for our current purposes, let's look at these verses in light of God's love for us instead of our love for each other.

> "Love is patient, love is kind. It does not envy, it does not boast, it is not proud. It is not rude, it is not self-seeking, it is not easily angered, it keeps no record of wrongs. Love does not delight in evil but rejoices with the truth. It always protects, always trusts, always hopes, always perseveres. Love never fails." (NIV)

In your walk of faith so far, what phrases describing God's love in the verses above have the most meaning for you? _____

_____

_____

_____

Here are the words that are especially meaningful to me from various translations: "not self-seeking . . . keeps no record of wrongs" (NIV); "does not demand its own way . . . not irritable" (NLT); "puts up with anything" (MSG); "endures long and is patient and kind . . . does not act unbecomingly . . . is ever ready to believe the best of every person, its hopes are fadeless under all circumstances . . . never fails—never fades out or becomes obsolete or comes to an end" (AMP). This is a type of love that is completely foreign to us and that we do not experience from those we share this world with, even other Christians. We also fail to give this type of love to anyone, even those we care about the most. The Bible is clear from beginning to end that God's first and foremost thought toward us is love—the kind of love we just read about. Everything else that he thinks or does is permeated by his utterly unselfish love for each of us, a love that is directed outward toward us rather than inward toward himself. The ultimate expression of this love was his gift of salvation through the sacrifice of his Son, Jesus.

But there are many other actions that God directs toward us that stem from his great love for us. In Job 10:12, Job says that God's unfailing love meant showing him kindness and preserving his life by his care, watching over his spirit and guarding every breath that he took. Isaiah 64:4–5a reminds us that God acts on behalf of us and works for us, welcoming and coming to the help of those who follow him. And, in 2 Peter 3:9, we see one example of God's extraordinary patience ("long-suffering", AMP) with all of mankind, even delaying the end of this world and the coming of his eternal kingdom so that more people will be included (" . . . restraining himself . . . giving everyone space and time to change", MSG). These actions (showing kindness, preserving life, watching over, guarding, acting on behalf of, working for, welcoming, helping, and patience) are just a few of the by-products of God's perfect love that thinks of others first and wants what is best for those he loves.

This brings us to God's goodness. In Jeremiah 29:11, God says that he has plans for us "for good, and not for disaster, to give . . . a future and a hope" (NLT). This much-quoted verse helps us to feel secure and protected when we embark on new adventures like graduations and weddings, but what does it really mean from God's perspective? To understand God's "good" for us, we have to look further. Another often quoted and often misunderstood verse, Romans 8:28, helps us to catch a glimpse of God's perspective: "And we know that in all things God works for *the good* of those who love him, who have been called according to his purpose" (NIV, emphasis mine). God's inherent goodness means that he sometimes acts in ways that we might not label as good. You see, goodness is not "feel-goodness". We want God's good for us to *feel* good, but that's not how God looks at things. God is interested in our long-range good and in fulfilling *his* purpose in us. He is the only one who can take the bad parts of living in an imperfect world and turn them to good that results in growth and fulfillment of his purpose in our lives. We have to trust his perfect love for us, which includes his perspective on goodness, in order to reconcile his willingness to allow us to sometimes experience deep pain even though he has deep concern for us. Once again, we cannot separate any of God's character traits from all of the others and expect to understand fully. God's thoughts toward us are always good whether we always feel good or not.

Beyond these basic thoughts of God toward all of us, the Bible also makes it clear that God cares personally for each one of us. In an earlier chapter, we looked at Matthew 6:25-32 and saw that we don't need to worry about food or clothing or any other earthly care because God knows all of our daily needs, caring deeply about them and providing for us. We also see in Matthew 10:30 that "even the very hairs of your head are all numbered" (NIV). Now that's personal care! Most of us have experienced some form of failure by others to properly or consistently care for our needs, whether physical or emotional. But God's care is constant and individual for each of us, overflowing from a heart that is not selfish, begrudging, or stingy in any way but instead generous and understanding (see Matthew 7:9-11 and Luke 11:11-13).

The greatest example of God's personal care for us is his gift of the Holy Spirit, who is described in various scriptures as a comforter, encourager, counselor, and advocate (a word which combines both comfort and counsel). The Greek word used in John 14:16-18 by Jesus as he tells his disciples that he will be leaving and the Holy Spirit will be coming is *Paracletos*, which means "one called alongside to help". He is described as " . . . another Friend so that you will always have someone with you" (MSG) and as " . . . Comforter (Counselor, Helper, Intercessor, Advocate, Strengthener and Standby)" (AMP). The Holy Spirit is on our side, always working *for* us and *with* us, always standing *by* us. As 2 Corinthians 1:3 says, God as Holy Spirit is the "source of all comfort" (NLT), which means he gives us strength, encouragement, and hope in the midst of trials and suffering. His presence is a definitive indicator of God's thoughts toward us.

Perhaps the most important work of the Holy Spirit is described in Philippians 1:6: " . . . he who began a good work in you will carry it on to completion . . ." (NIV). The work in each of us that Jesus started with his death on the cross is being carried on by the presence of the Holy Spirit in us. Whether or not we feel that we are making progress in our Christian walk or accomplishing anything worthwhile, we know that God won't give up on us and promises to complete the work *he* started in each of us. In fact, as *The Message* translation puts it, " . . . God who started this great work in you (will) keep at it and bring it to a *flourishing* finish . . ." (emphasis mine).

The Bible also gives us two very powerful and practical images to describe God that help us to further understand his thoughts toward us. As examples that draw on our daily experiences, they are particularly helpful in bridging the gap between how God thinks and how we think. The images of God as a father and God as a shepherd give us concrete ways of developing a picture of God that we can relate to. We will look at God as a father first.

Many passages in the Bible make it clear that God is a father to each of us. In John 20:17, Jesus tells Mary Magdalene that God is *her* father as well as his; and 1 John 3:1 reminds us " . . . how very much our Father loves us, for he calls us his children . . ." (NLT). But whether we find this idea of God as our father to be positive or not often depends on our own experiences with earthly fathers, all of whom display fatherly qualities in varying degrees of imperfection. Since I have never been a father, I asked my husband to help me come up with a list of father qualities: things that all fathers are called to do, that some exhibit well, and that God embodies perfectly. While not an exhaustive list, we determined that fathers are the God–appointed leaders of their families, responsible to care for, provide for, and protect. They are to teach and discipline their children, seeking God's best for each one. Fathers should be humble, honest, forgiving, comforting, and encouraging. They are called to be an example and to train, direct, or point their children in the right direction according to how each child is designed by God (see Proverbs 22:6 and *You and Your Child* by Charles R. Swindoll[4]). Look at how Deuteronomy 6:6-9 describes the daily involvement and attention to details that God expects fathers to have: "Write these commandments that I've given you today on your hearts. Get them inside of you and then get them inside your children. Talk about them wherever you are, sitting at home or walking in the street; talk about them from the time you get up in the morning to when you fall into bed at night. Tie them on your hands and foreheads as a reminder; inscribe them on the doorposts of your homes and on your city gates" (MSG).

A Biblical example of a father who exhibited at least some of these qualities is the story in Luke 15:11-32 of the prodigal son. Most of the time, our attention when reading this story is on the sins and repentance of the son; but this story provides us with a great picture of a father who watched and waited for his wayward son with constant love and patience. He welcomed his son with forgiveness, accepting him wholeheartedly and giving him support and encouragement to grow. *The Amplified New Testament* says that the father "was moved with pity *and* tenderness [for him]", qualities that earthly fathers often struggle to express.

A good father thinks of his children as full human beings, taking note of their feelings and their individual abilities as he is daily involved with them. A Jewish scholar in Biblical times said that a good father should "push them away with the left hand and draw them near with the right hand"[5]—an ideal balance between firmness and affection. This is the kind of father that God is, as we see in Proverbs 3:12 that "the LORD corrects those he loves, just as a father corrects a child in whom he delights" (NLT). It is important for us to remember that, as a perfect father, God's discipline is a sign of his deep love for us and evidence or proof that we are his children. As

Hebrews 12:6 tells us, "the Lord corrects *and* disciplines every one whom He loves, and He punishes, even scourges, every son whom He accepts *and* welcomes to His heart *and* cherishes" (AMP). God as father accepts us, cherishes us, and welcomes us to his heart! And his discipline is always corrective and instructive, leading to wholesome and beneficial results because his discipline is perfect and designed to produce a perfect response. This is truly a father-figure whose thoughts toward us can be fully trusted.

The second image that we have of God in the Bible is that of a shepherd, a picture which Americans in the twenty-first century are less acquainted with than those who originally read the Old and New Testaments. But it is definitely worth our time to examine this image because it is so rich in meaning for our understanding of God's thoughts toward us.

Look up the following verses and list all of the things a shepherd does for his sheep. Take your time and soak up all of the ways that these descriptions apply to God as a shepherd (try using several versions of the Bible again).

Isaiah 40:11 _____
_____
_____

Psalm 23 _____
_____
_____
_____

John 10:1-15 _____
_____
_____
_____
_____

I hope you received a blessing as you looked at these passages! To summarize what you found: we see that a shepherd is gentle and has deep concern for his sheep, even knowing each one by name. Being a shepherd requires watchfulness and tenderness as he goes before them, calls to them, strengthens the weak and sick, gathers and protects, and gives his best to the sheep. The shepherd leads the sheep in paths that offer safety and well-being where they can lie down in contented and secure rest. The shepherd's rod (an instrument of authority) is used for counting, guiding, rescuing, and protecting; and, together with his staff (an instrument of support), brings comfort or reassurance to the sheep. We also see that God as Jesus, the good shepherd, is the "gate" across the doorway of the sheepfold (thus providing protection) and that he has a deep knowledge of each of us ("I know my sheep, and my sheep know me", John 10:14, NIV). In Matthew 18:12-14, we discover that God cares so deeply for each of us that he rejoices over every single person when we are saved. In fact, he even goes looking for us and searches until he finds us!

Oh, that we could begin to grasp the ramifications of God's thoughts toward us! And that we could allow those God-thoughts to transform our view of ourselves and our ability to be used by God. To say that each one of us matters to God is a huge understatement, but it is something that we must try to believe and act on. When we are inundated with doubt and other negative thoughts about ourselves from Satan and our circumstances, we must choose to believe what God thinks about us and recognize what he has done and is doing on our behalf. It is important for us to remember what the Bible teaches us about God's thoughts toward us in order to combat the attacks from the enemy on our self-esteem. "Scripture is a vast tapestry of God's creating, saving, and blessing ways in this world. The great names in the plot . . . can be intimidating to ordinary, random individuals . . . our unimpressive, very ordinary lives make us feel like outsiders . . . we conclude that we are . . . unfit to participate in the big story."[6] Stories like Ruth, Samuel, Saul, and David make it possible "for each of us to understand ourselves, however ordinary or 'out of it', as irreplaceable in the full telling of God's story. We count—every last one of us—and what we do counts . . . We don't have to fit into prefabricated moral or mental or religious boxes before we are admitted into the company of God—we are taken seriously just as we are and given a place in his story."[7]

Through my own experiences with low self-esteem, guilt, and depression surrounding the closure of our business and the subsequent life-changes, I found that I had to *choose* each day to climb out of my feelings and base my outlook *only* on God's thoughts toward me rather than my own or the thoughts of others. In order to make it through each day, it was necessary for me to focus on God's love and personal care for me, his goodness, and his actions as a good shepherd and a perfect father. And I also had to believe that God was still at work in me, despite all evidence to the contrary, and that his work would result in good regardless of the appearance of evil in me, in other people, and in the world around me. As Peterson says, "God, it turns out, does not require good people in order to do good work. He can and does work within us in whatever moral and spiritual condition he finds us. God . . . does some of his best work using the most unlikely people."[8] Although today I don't struggle as much with low self-esteem as I did previously, I still have to choose on a regular basis to trust God's thoughts toward me. I believe that *most* people need to do the same, and I pray that you will allow God's thoughts toward you to transform your thoughts about yourself and enable you to step out in faith to be used by him.

Which thoughts of God toward you are the easiest for you to trust and why? _____

_____

_____

_____

Which thoughts of God toward you are the hardest for you to trust and why? _____

_____

_____

_____

What specific action or choice can you make on a daily basis that will help you to trust God's thoughts toward you instead of your own or others'? _____

_____

_____

_____

Lesson 5

Trusting God's Grace

Trusting God's thoughts toward us and truly believing what he says about us instead of what we or others feel places us in a better position to trust God's grace, which shows up in many different forms throughout our lives. Sometimes we recognize it, and sometimes we don't; and sometimes we accept it, sometimes we don't. God's grace doesn't always look like a gift, and this is where we especially have to employ faith in the process of accepting it.

In the dictionary, grace is defined as favor or good will, mercy, clemency, pardon. In the Bible, we see that grace is God's voluntary and loving favor given to us—unearned and undeserved—coming only from his mercy and love. We also see that grace is something we *experience*, which makes it harder to define. It is "an insubstantial invisible reality that permeates all that we are, think, speak and do".[1] God's concept of grace is not a noun that can be objectively defined. Instead, God himself has become "the verbing of a noun".[2]

In the Old Testament, using a particular name for God (there were many different ones used) had specific meaning and implied unique characteristics about God and his nature, a certain way in which

God related to his creation. In Exodus 34:5-7, we see that God calls himself gracious and compassionate or full of grace and mercy. These same two words are pared together and repeated over and over in the Old Testament to help us get the picture of how God always responds to us. He "verbs" grace by being compassionate and merciful. In Isaiah 30:18-19, we also see that God is "waiting around to be gracious to you . . . Cry for help and you'll find it's grace and more grace" (MSG).

As we move to the New Testament, Romans 5 reminds us that Christ's love is grounded in God's free grace and not the result of any inherent goodness in us, lavished upon us in spite of our undesirable character (v. 5). We also see that the effect of God's grace is infinitely greater for good than Adam's sin was for evil (v. 15) but that, to be effective, God's grace must be received (v. 18). The Bible also gives us a picture of the different forms that God's grace takes, which are endless because grace has become a verb rather than a noun. I want to look at four of these manifestations in greater depth: original salvation grace, grace when we sin, grace that is sufficient for whatever we face, and grace in relating to one another.

I don't have a rich experience with God's saving grace. When I first trusted God at the age of four to save me from eternal death, I had not yet acquired a long list of sins or any understanding of the shame and guilt that could have characterized my life if I had not chosen to follow God. While I do believe that I actually became a Christian at that tender age, I was in danger of experiencing what Dietrich Bonhoeffer called "cheap grace": grace without the cross. All but the first four years of my life has been wholly permeated by the concept of grace, so I struggle to understand what it would be like to live any part of life without it. And, while I have no regrets for the privilege of coming to God at such a young age, I have had to learn from others about the depths of God's saving grace and the effects it can have on a life. My *Celebrate Recovery* friends at church have a different story to tell, and their complete immersion in God's grace (and the changes it has brought about in their lives) is inspiring to see and share. Adults who are new Christians always bring a refreshing dimension to my walk of faith because they have a perspective I have never experienced.

What is your story of God's *saving* grace? Do you have a firsthand experience of being saved from an active life of sin, or have you had to learn about this kind of grace from the experiences of others? __

_____

_____

_____

_____

_____

_____

One of the best-known passages in God's Word that helps us to understand his salvation grace is Ephesians 2:4-9:

> "But God is so rich in mercy, and he loved us so much, that even though we were dead because of our sins, he gave us life when he raised Christ from the dead. (It is only by God's grace that you have been saved!) For he raised us from the dead along with Christ and seated us with him in the heavenly realms because we are united with Christ Jesus. So God can point to us in all future ages as examples of the incredible wealth of his grace and kindness toward us, as shown in all he has done for us who are united with Christ Jesus. God saved you by his grace when you believed. And you can't take credit for this; it is a gift from God. Salvation is not a reward for the good things we have done, so none of us can boast about it." (NLT)

It is clear that God did not save us because of but rather in spite of what he saw in us. We don't become Christians as the result of our effort, ability, intelligent choice, or act of service, but by God's grace alone: "He did all this on his own, with no help from us!" (MSG). Romans 11:6 further helps us to understand that grace cannot include works and cannot be earned but only accepted: " . . . grace would no longer be grace—it would be meaningless" (AMP). In Romans 5, we also see the giving aspect of God's grace, as God has "thrown open his door to us" (v. 2, MSG) and has "put his love on the line for us by offering his Son in sacrificial death while we were of no use whatever to him" (v. 8, MSG). *The Message* translates verse 5 like this: "we can't round up enough containers to hold everything God generously pours into our lives", and another version reminds us that God's free gift operates on a different principle than we would expect, as "His grace is out of all proportion to the fall of man" (v. 15, AMP).

In understanding God's salvation grace, we have to remember that all of God's character traits operate in conjunction with each other: his grace, mercy, love, holiness, and righteousness are interconnected. God's mercy is the compassion that moved him to provide a Savior, and his love is the motivation behind everything he does toward man. But grace couldn't operate until God's holiness and righteousness were satisfied by a sufficient answer to sin. This is further evidence that grace rules out all human merit because no amount of human effort can provide a sufficient answer to sin. Only God could satisfy the requirements created by his own character. All we can do is admit our own insufficiency and accept his free gift of grace in providing a suitable sacrifice that covers every possibility of sin in our lives and bridges the gap between ourselves and a holy God.

After we have trusted God's grace to provide eternal salvation and restore our broken relationship with him, it doesn't take long for us to discover that this new position unfortunately does not guarantee that we will stop sinning. We can almost immediately lament along with the apostle Paul: "I do not understand what I do. For what I want to do I do not do, but what I hate I do . . . I know that nothing good lives in me, that is, in my sinful nature. For I have the desire to do what is good, but I cannot carry it out. For what I do is not the good I want to do; no, the evil I do not want to do—this I keep on doing" (Romans 7:15, 18-19, NIV). And we learn that this lament will last for the rest of our earthly lives. This is where we must learn to trust God's grace on a daily basis to cover our sins, and this is where it gets tricky.

The Bible makes it clear that all humans sin, Christians and non-Christians alike. Even after we have received God's provision for our eternal separation from him, we all do things that separate us from him temporarily. God's saving grace gives us a position "in Christ" that allows God to look at us through his Son and see no sin; but, because we all continue to sin after we are saved, we must daily restore this position by appropriating the grace that God provides to cover every sin. If we do not trust this grace whenever we sin, Christian growth will not occur. We cannot grow if we are still trying to overcome sin on our own; we will continue to be "stuck" in salvation grace—saved from eternal separation from God but lacking any power to overcome sin on a daily basis.

The role of grace when we sin is hard for us to put our fingers on. If God will always forgive us through his grace, then it's easy for sin to not seem very serious. On the other hand, sometimes our sin is so great that we don't know when to continue to seek cleansing and when to accept grace and move on. We have trouble not engaging "the law" and legalism in defining what sin is while moving to a place of fully understanding the seriousness of sin so that we can better receive God's grace fully. Singer and author Michael Card refers to this as "violent grace".[3] He reminds us that, while we have to make the choice to obey God everyday, it is God's grace that both gives us that ability and also covers our failures. Our walk of faith is utterly dependent upon grace.

Romans 5-8 provides an in-depth look at the contrast between following the law and walking in grace. The whole section is worth spending some time in, but a couple of verses are especially meaningful in helping us understand the role of God's grace when we sin. Romans 5:20 tells us that the role of the law is to show us our need for God. The "rules" God wants us to follow can sometimes seem like a ladder that we have to climb to get to him—a ladder we have all failed to climb repeatedly. But the role of grace is to lift us above the ladder and take us directly to God, giving us the ability to follow the rules out of love instead of necessity. Grace means that, when we stumble, we don't fall all the way back to the bottom of the ladder but only into the arms of Jesus and God's grace.

Romans 6:14 further encourages us by helping us to see that grace not only covers our sin but actually *enables* us to resist sinning, something the law has no power to do. There is freedom when we live in God's grace. When we mingle legalism with grace, we are actually distorting grace and making it meaningless, as Galatians 2:21 addresses: we do not want to "treat God's gracious gift as something of minor importance and defeat its very purpose . . . set aside *and* invalidate *and* frustrate *and* nullify the grace . . ." (AMP). Trusting God's grace when we sin is a constant balancing act between appropriating his grace and power as we strive to avoid sinning and accepting his grace and moving on when we fail. This frees us to experience other aspects of God's grace in our walk of faith.

The older we get, the more we realize that everyone experiences times of difficulty: losses, financial setbacks, sicknesses, and lots of other things. As Christians, we understand that this is part of living in a fallen world where sin is still present even though ultimately defeated. It doesn't take long for us to need God's words in 2 Corinthians 12:9: "My grace is sufficient for you, for my power is made perfect in weakness" (NIV). But what does the sufficiency of God's grace really look like? Or better yet, what does it *feel* like? When I am hurting and needing grace, what can I expect to receive? Because we are all on different journeys with God, the answer to those questions may not be the same for everyone. That is when it becomes essential that we believe what God has said and learn to trust the sufficiency of God's grace regardless of what it looks or feels like.

I learned 2 Cor. 12:9 early in my adult walk of faith by watching someone close to me rely on those words time and time again to walk through the darkness of chronic depression. Trusting that God's grace was sufficient meant getting out of bed each day and going through the motions of everyday life, relying on God's strength to do just that, until once again feeling like really living. More recently, I have watched my mother learn the sufficiency of God's grace as she walks through the uncharted course of life on her own after the death of my father and the end of fifty-six years of togetherness. She has to trust that God's grace is sufficient even when it doesn't *feel* sufficient—or maybe especially then.

I have also learned through my own version of brokenness and trials that God's grace truly is sufficient, though the journey to experiencing that belief point was neither easy nor guaranteed. I think that's because the rest of 2 Cor. 12:9 is not something we want to accept. No one wants to be weak, but we cannot experience the sufficiency of God's grace without the brokenness.

Carol Hamblet Adams has written a book that helps us to embrace our brokenness—whatever it is—and recognize what God can do, not *despite* our brokenness but *because* of it. I recently read *My Beautiful Broken Shell* again after a few years since the first time I read it. In her analogy of the similarities between a broken seashell and our broken lives, Adams reminds us of many of the aspects of God's sufficient grace: we are not completely crushed by our trials; we find courage and strength; we learn to see the beauty beyond the brokenness; we learn faith and inspire others; we experience God's presence and receive hope in times of despair, light in times of darkness, patience in times of suffering; and, most of all, we discover that, regardless of our level of brokenness, we are still whole and complete in God's sight.[4] Only God's grace is sufficient enough to accomplish that.

When have you experienced the sufficiency of God's grace? What circumstances or trials were you experiencing? _____

_____

_____

When have you struggled to find God's grace to be sufficient? What was the result, or are you still struggling? _____

_____

_____

Read 1 Peter 5:10-12. How do you feel about Peter's belief that suffering is actually part of God's grace for us? _____

_____

_____

_____

These last verses are encouraging to me because, when we are faced with suffering, we usually tend to believe that God has removed himself from us and that his grace is absent. The enemy is very adept at getting us to focus on the suffering and to feel that we are all alone in our experience. We do everything we can to get rid of the suffering. Peter encourages us to stand firm in God's grace so we can trust God's words from 2 Cor. 12:9: "My grace is all you need" (NLT). Trusting the sufficiency of God's grace means relying completely on him and him alone no matter what life brings our way and embracing the trials as part of God's presence and work in our lives instead of trying to escape the brokenness. Hebrews 4:16 reminds us that we have the privilege of coming "boldly to the throne of our gracious God" where "we will find grace to help us when we need it most" (NLT).

When I think about the fourth manifestation of God's grace—how we relate to one another—I cringe. I am hopelessly truth-oriented, and pretty much nothing about grace comes naturally to me. Every generation seems to err on one side or the other of these two. Many in my children's generation lean toward grace and stumble over truth, whereas my parents' generation was strong on truth and weak on grace. As a result of my upbringing and my natural bent, I have had no problem recognizing or walking in truth; but I have had a lifelong struggle to pursue grace and to look at all of life through the eyes of grace and not just truth. I have failed to achieve balance countless times, and I receive encouragement when my attempts fall short by remembering the words of John 1:14 that remind me that only Jesus achieved the perfect balance of grace and truth. In fact, it's our humanness that even places truth and grace as opposites just because *we* can't find the balance! Embodied in Christ, these two concepts come alive in perfect balance. As my brother says, Jesus wasn't 50% truth and 50% grace but rather 100% of each.

So, with Jesus as our example, what do we need to learn about grace in order to extend it to others? For some of us with a natural bent toward truth, this may be a longer answer than for others. It may also be a painful answer since most of our best learning takes place through difficult circumstances. For me, my own struggle with faith and my experience of a lack of grace from others were God's tools to begin building more grace into my relationships. He is still working, and I will always be learning; but I am a little further down the road than I used to be.

When we closed our business, I spent several months unsuccessfully looking for employment and trying to make sense of God's purposes in all that had happened. During the same time period, God was bringing to an end a thirty-eight-year association with our church, resulting in the loss of ministry and most of our long-term friendships. As I struggled for the first time to find faith and to keep believing that God was still at work, I came to the end of my abilities, my spiritual gifts, and my self-esteem. I began to see myself in a different light, which eventually led to me being able to see others in a little different light. I learned what it was like to walk in someone's shoes who lacks faith. I learned what it was like to be deceived even with the spiritual gift of discernment. I learned that everyone struggles with something, even me. The result? The seeds of compassion were planted in me and began to grow. I'll never be naturally compassionate, and I don't have the gift of mercy; but I'm trying to move in the right direction more deliberately than before.

Sometimes our life experiences and personalities affect our ability to *give* grace, and sometimes they affect our ability to *receive* grace. I have discovered that my own neediness affects my ability to give grace to others, but I have also seen the effect that a lack of grace from *others* can have on my ability to receive and accept *God's* grace. Not only do we have to choose to give grace to others, but we also have to continue to trust God's grace regardless of how others respond to us. I am so thankful that God's grace is always lavished upon us regardless of how well we fulfill his call to exhibit grace toward one another.

In our effort to fully understand and trust God's grace, each of us will reach a point where we must answer the "So what?" question. If God's grace in its many forms is freely given and always available to me, what does trusting it look like for me? How can I be sure that I am accepting God's grace when it appears? And what effect should that grace have on me? In other words, what should I be doing differently because of grace? This is when we encounter a disturbing verse in Hebrews 12:15: "See to it that no one misses the grace of God . . ." (NIV). Other versions imply the same danger: " . . . so that none of you fails to receive the grace of God" (NLT) and "Make sure no one gets left out of God's generosity" (MSG).

Now that scares me: I don't want to get left out or miss God's grace in any way.

In discussing what it means to live a grace-filled Christian life, Eugene Peterson has created the term "acquired passivity" to describe how we can make sure we don't miss God's grace in a culture that persistently denies grace and focuses on manipulation and control to get ahead and find purpose. We don't get to control what grace is or what it looks like. God made that decision for us and didn't come up with a "Plan B". Therefore, grace is "not what we do, it is what we participate in. But we cannot participate apart from a willed passivity, entering into a giving ourselves up to what is previous to us, the presence and action of God in Christ that is other than us . . . abandoning the shores of self, where we think we know where we stand and where if we just try hard enough we can be in control."[5] Peterson reminds us that grace is a wide ocean that we enter only by diving in. Only when we accept grace on its own terms do we get to experience "the soul-transforming implications of grace—a comprehensive, foundational reorientation from living anxiously by my wits and muscle to living effortlessly in the world of God's active presence."[6] This, then, is how we learn to trust God's grace: by getting to the end of ourselves. Perhaps that is why it seems that grace is best experienced by those who have failed the most; they have already reached the end of themselves and their efforts.

To illustrate, allow me to share a very personal story of God's grace. I have learned a lot about grace from one of my sons, who is a recovering addict. Now I'm not going to tell you which son or what his addiction is because that isn't my story to tell (though I do have his permission to talk about it). Suffice it to say that, in our post-modern American culture, there are many more addiction options available than in the past and Satan is still alive and well and willing to use whatever he can to sidetrack God's children. You see, my son's addiction came years after he had given his life to God and chosen to live for him. Unlike many other people whose addictions occurred "before Christ" and Christ saved them *from* the addiction, my son has had to not only deal with the addiction on a daily basis but also his failure to walk as God wanted him to and the effect the addiction has had on his relationship with God. I will talk more about other issues that we have faced related to this addiction in later chapters, but for now I want to focus on grace.

My son's entire being is permeated by grace, which has become a definite distinctive trait of who he is. He has experienced God's grace in the form of forgiveness too many times to count. Rather than just being able to leave the darkness behind as something that happened "before Christ", he has had to regularly stop beating himself up for failing to do what a Christian is *supposed* to do and appropriate God's grace to overcome Satan's deception and power. He has had to trust that God's grace is sufficient and all he needs when the addiction calls and the enemy pummels his self-esteem— when he is busy working through and embracing the brokenness in Christian counseling and putting accountability partners in place instead of living a carefree young adult life. He has had to trust God's grace whether others choose to give him grace or not. He will spend the rest of his life needing to trust God's grace for every day.

But here's the exciting result of his choice to dive into the wide ocean of God's grace in its many forms instead of continuing active participation in the addiction: my son is one of the most compassionate young adults I know, giving grace freely and feeling God's call on his life to use his experience with addiction to make a difference in the lives of others. He has decided that his life must embody what Titus 2:11-12 and 2 Corinthians 6:1 both speak to: God's grace should make a difference, affecting what we say and do and encouraging right living and grace-giving to others. Otherwise, we squander what God has given us and nullify its purpose beyond eternal salvation.

Through the grace God has given to us, we must become vessels of his grace to those around us. Because of his experiences, my son has a head start on the rest of us in this area.

Eugene Peterson says grace is "underlying and comprehensive God-giftedness . . . the basic giftedness of everything God is and does". With this picture of grace, it is easy to see why how we treat others matters. Our extension of grace toward others is how we enter in and participate in the world of God's grace, how we "verb" God's grace into the lives of others. We provide a visible form for the invisibilities of grace: like a pail and water, we are the container that holds the precious content of God's grace. Only when we choose to trust God's grace in its many forms and rely on it as fully sufficient for all of our needs are we in a position to be an extension of God's grace in its many forms to those around us.[7] I'm still learning; but I want to be a pail that pours generously in direct proportion to the pouring of God's grace over me.

What factors affect your ability to trust God's grace to cover your daily sins? _____

_____

_____

Read 1 John 1:9. How does this verse help you to trust God's grace?

_____

_____

_____

Is there one area of your life where you need to reach the end of yourself or embrace the brokenness? How will this help you to trust God's grace? _____

_____

_____

_____

Name one relationship in your life where you need to grow in your expression of God's grace. What is one thing from this chapter that you can focus on that will affect your next response in this relationship? _____

_____

_____

_____

Lesson 6

Trusting God's Purposes

Let's start this chapter with complete honesty: most of us have struggled at one time or another to trust God's purposes. In fact, most of us have struggled to even *know* God's purposes, much less *trust* them. The apostle Paul addressed this in Romans 11:33-36, pointing out that, because of God's great riches and wisdom and knowledge, "How impossible it is for us to understand his decisions and his ways!" (NLT). Some of our experiences in life don't make sense from our perspective, and we have a hard time getting to a point of trust apart from understanding (which is, of course, what *real* faith is!).

Describe a time when you have struggled to trust God's purposes. What made if difficult for you? _____

_____

_____

_____

_____

I have found, through much hard work (and trial and error), that trusting God's purposes involves stepping outside of *my* perspective and trying to look at life from *God's* perspective. I have also discovered that trusting God's purposes cannot be separated from knowing and trusting the other parts of him: his sovereignty, his love, his thoughts toward me, his grace and mercy, and everything else that his Word tells me about his character. Truly believing what the Bible teaches me about God's heart and motivation helps me to trust his purposes when they don't match my purposes or seem to make any sense. So . . . remembering all we have discussed so far . . . let's get started.

Trusting God's purposes begins with the truth outlined for us in Ephesians 1:4-11:

> "Long before he laid down earth's foundations, he had us in mind, had settled on us as the focus of his love, to be made whole and holy by his love. Long, long ago he decided to adopt us into his family through Jesus Christ. (What pleasure he took in planning this!) He wanted us to enter into the celebration of his lavish gift-giving by the hand of his beloved Son . . . He thought of everything, provided for everything we could possibly need, letting us in on the plans he took such delight in making. He set it all out before us in Christ, a long-range plan in which everything would be brought together and summed up in him, everything in deepest heaven, everything on planet earth." (MSG)

God has an *overall* purpose for every part of his creation, and we are a part of that purpose. But we are only a *part*.

God is all about relationship, and his overall purpose is to bring *everything* in creation into meaningful relationship with himself and each other under Christ. We need to remember that this purpose can NEVER be thwarted regardless of the evil that Satan brings or the present view we have of a world that lacks sense and is in a state of confusion. "God's purposes are worked out in confrontation and revelation, in judgment and salvation, but they *are* worked out."[1] In 2 Peter 3:8-9, Peter also reminds us that God isn't in a hurry to accomplish his overall purpose but is willing to patiently wait for every single part of his creation to have the opportunity to be a part of that purpose. What God has planned for all of his creation is far beyond our planning abilities and far more purposeful than anything we can imagine because it is an *eternal* purpose: "For everything comes from him and exists by his power and is intended for his glory" (Romans 11:36a, NLT). In order to begin trusting God's purposes, I need to trust his overall purpose of meaningful relationship and be a willing participant in bringing him the glory he is due.

The next step in trusting God's purposes is to focus on what the Bible tells us about the characteristics of those purposes. Look up the following verses and list the words used to describe God's purposes, plans, or ways:

Psalm 25:10 _____

_____

Psalm 33:11 _____

_____

Psalm 77:13 _____

_____

Psalm 145:17 _____

_____

Proverbs 4:11 _____

_____

Proverbs 4:26 _____

_____

Habakkuk 3:6 _____

_____

Revelation 15:3 _____

_____

In these verses, we find many characteristics of God's ways (purposes) that should help us in our effort to trust them: God's purposes are just and true, they are eternal or everlasting, they are holy and righteous, and they are always loving and faithful. In the Bible, "heart" refers to the center of the human spirit from which emotions, thought, motivations, courage, and action all come. We are told that the purposes of *God's* heart stand firm through all generations and can never be shaken. God is completely consistent, so we can count on him to lead us in "straight" paths. This does not mean that everything will always be smooth (from *our* perspective); but we can trust God to lead us in paths that are right (from *his* perspective): "I'm writing out clear directions to Wisdom Way; I'm drawing a map to Righteous Road" (Proverbs 4:11, MSG). When I am tempted to question God's purposes or wonder why he does things a certain way, it is helpful to remind myself what his Word tells me about the kind of leader he is and the "heart" that guides everything he does.

Another very important step in the process of trusting God's purposes is to recognize the contrast between our very limited perspective of just about everything and God's overall "big picture" view of *absolutely* everything. If you remember anything from elementary school science, you know that planet earth is a very small part of God's complete creation; and that doesn't even address the small portion of earth that each of us resides on in comparison to the whole planet. We simply do not have a proper perspective, in any sense of the word, to even have an *opinion* on what God's purposes should be, much less any *control* over them. This was God's message through Isaiah: "My thoughts are nothing like your thoughts . . . and my ways are far beyond anything you could imagine. For just as the heavens are higher than the earth, so my ways are higher than your ways and my thoughts higher than your thoughts" (Isaiah 55:8–9, NLT). For God, everything is connected (which includes a vast array of things we don't even know about), and he is always working in every situation from this overall perspective of connectedness. From our limited perspective, it is foolish for us to try to fit God into our mold (to try and make his plans and purposes conform to ours) or to act as if we know what God is thinking and planning. As Proverbs 19:21 tells us and as we were encouraged to do in the book *Experiencing God*,[2] we should be trying to fit into *God's* plans and to join what he's already doing: "Many are the plans in a man's heart, but it is the LORD's purpose that prevails" (NIV).

Most of the time, we humans have to fight a self-centered viewpoint. We tend to believe that anything we are experiencing has isolated purposes for us alone. We forget that if our story is part of God's overall story, then "God is the larger context and plot in which our stories find themselves".[3] It's not just about us, but also about God using *our* story connected with *someone else's* story to complete *his* story. Which means that " . . . the stuff of our ordinary and often disappointing human experience . . . is the very stuff that God uses to create and save and give hope . . . nothing is unusable by God. He uses everything and everybody as material for his work . . ."[4] It also means that " . . . nothing in human experience can be omitted or slighted if we decide to take God seriously and respond to him believingly. God and God's ways provide the comprehensive plot and sovereign action . . . but human beings—every last man and woman of us, including every last detail involved in our daily living—are invited and honored participants in all of it. There are no spectator seats provided for the drama . . . no 'bench' for incompetent players."[5] When life doesn't make sense to us, it is good to remember whose story is being told and to recognize the privilege that we have to be included in the telling of that story.

Part of this new and better perspective is to see beyond the present and realize that God's purposes may unfold over the course of our lives and not at the moment we desire. We tend to be very short-sighted, not patient enough to wait for God's purposes to make sense. And we also tend to forget that God will use *each* of us in different ways to accomplish his purpose in the lives of *all* of us. What we are trying to make isolated sense out of may be something God plans to use in the lives of others rather than just for *our* growth. With all that happened to Job, God was growing him while at the same time providing an example for all future generations. It was impossible for Job to fully comprehend that perspective while in the midst of such seemingly meaningless and purposeless suffering. God never explained the suffering to Job, but simply asked him to trust God's purposes—which he would never completely see in his lifetime.

When my husband and I got married, we were very young and quite naïve. We both very much wanted our marriage to reflect God's purposes and be used for his glory in every way. As a younger Christian, Ron wanted to model his walk after mine and other Christians who were further down the road than him; and I thought I had a pretty good perspective from which to help him along in that process since I had been a Christian for eighteen years already. You can feel the disaster coming, can't you? While Ron tried to be like me and I tried to make him more like me, we both thought we understood God's purposes for our marriage and how God would use us. Our motives were pure, but our methods were way off base. At the end of our first year of marriage, we fortunately had listened enough to what God was saying to recognize what was wrong with our plan. God's purpose for our marriage was not necessarily the same as *our* purpose, and his methods in reaching that purpose were most certainly not the same as ours. I had to step back and allow God to grow Ron in his way and his time and recognize that some of my husband's most change-worthy traits (from my limited perspective) weren't important from God's perspective. In fact, changing these traits wasn't even necessary in order for God to use him. Ron also had to discover enough about himself (and me) to recognize that he didn't need to be just like someone else in order for God to have a plan for him. God had put two very different people together for a lifetime of *his* purposes, and we are thankful that our usefulness in those purposes was not decided once and for all by our naïveté and our need to grow in certain areas. And, while we still haven't experienced all of God's purposes for our marriage, over the years we have seen numerous ways that God has used our uniqueness as individuals with different gifts, as well as our oneness as husband and wife, to be a "sermon" in the lives of others. This was a prayer of ours that was sung at our wedding, and God has answered that prayer many times in different ways to accomplish his purposes through us.[6]

One of the unique things about God that is different from us is his ability to see the entire "big picture" while at the same time caring for each individual person. This means that, while he has an overall purpose for everyone and sees everything as connected within his plan, he also has an individual purpose for each of us and works in our lives individually to guide us along the path he wants for us. Psalm 138:8 tells us that God "will fulfill his purpose for me" (NIV), and Proverbs 3:6 reminds us that "he's the one who will keep you on track" (MSG), removing the obstacles from your pathway and bringing you to your appointed goal—when you are working to accomplish *his* purposes. Trusting God's purposes for us individually involves trusting his heart and motives which are revealed to us throughout the Bible. Look up the following verses and list what they reveal about God's heart and motives:

Psalm 23:3 _____

_____

Jeremiah 29:11 _____

_____

Romans 8:28 _____

_____

These are all very familiar verses, but let's not miss what they are telling us about God's heart. Jeremiah 29:11 says that God has "plans for good and not for disaster, to give you a future and a hope" (NLT), and Psalm 23:3 says that he "guides us in paths of righteousness" (NIV). Righteousness is often translated as "prosperity" in the Bible. In the context of a shepherd leading his sheep in paths of safety and well-being, God can be trusted to guide in ways that cause us to be secure and prosperous. The obvious implication is that, when we fail to trust God's purposes, we are actually going against our own best interests. As Romans 8:28 tells us, "We are assured and know that

[God being a partner in their labor], all things work together and are [fitting into a plan] for good to those who love God and are called according to [His] design and purpose" (AMP). This means that God is always working in everything—not just isolated incidents—for what is good for us. He is not working to make us happy but rather to fulfill his purpose for us. If we read a little further in Romans 8, we discover what that purpose is: "the good" is that which conforms us to "the likeness of his Son" (v. 29, NIV). God is always interested in growing our character and our relationship with him. We can trust his purposes for us because he knows what is best for us; and we know he always has our best interests in mind.

In some ways, trusting God's purposes involves getting to the end of our own purposes. As twenty-first century Americans, we tend to try to accomplish our purposes before we rest in God's purposes. We try to better ourselves or "fix" everything before we trust God. But "God's great love and purposes for us are worked out in the messes, storms and sins, blue skies, daily work, and dreams of our common lives, working with us as we are and not as we should be."[7] Trusting God's purposes instead of our own "call(s) a halt to our various and futile attempts to make something of our lives, so that we can give our full attention to God—who God is and what *he* does to make something of us . . . (exposing) our total incapacity to find the meaning and completion of our lives on our own."[8] We simply don't have enough knowledge or wisdom to guide our own lives. The sooner we recognize this and trust God's purposes for us, the better off we will be. Unfortunately, this is not a lesson most of us learn once and for all; we must learn to trust God's purposes over and over as we are faced with circumstances that defy human understanding.

To help us in this lifelong learning curve, God gave us the story of Job. As mentioned earlier, Job never saw all of God's purposes for his suffering; but God still made it clear to Job that he expected a response of trust. In his words to Job and his friends, God's message to them and us is this: since we can't fully understand the workings of God's physical creation, we can't possibly understand his mind and character. If nature is beyond our grasp, then God's purposes may not be what we imagine either. God's actions do not depend on ours. He will do what he knows is best regardless of what we think is fair or what makes sense to us. Our job is not to question or seek to control the outcome but simply to "join in" where God's purposes are being worked out and trust those purposes to be the best solution. Eugene Peterson says that much of what God does is invisible and unnoticed, which is the opposite of what we are used to. "God's characteristic way of working is in quietness and through prayer . . . if we are conditioned to respond to noise and size, we will miss God's word and action."[9] Joining in where God is working involves listening for his voice above all of the other voices and trusting him to take what we call bad and make it good.

My personal experiences with trusting God's purposes have been some of my most difficult spiritual battles. As a logic-driven person, I want everything to make sense. Trusting God's purposes when they defy logic is a struggle for me. When we bought our retail business, we took a huge leap of faith in many ways because we believed beyond a shadow of doubt that it was God's will and that he was in it. We viewed the business as God's business, and we believed that it would be successful as a result. When the business failed less than four years later, I struggled with the concept that our faith was actually what had gotten us to this low point in our lives. I still struggle with this concept; but I am continuing to learn that God's purposes are not isolated to me (I am part of a bigger picture), that he is working for my good and what is best, and that the story he is telling is much more important than any of "my stories" because it is an eternal story.

Responding to my son's addiction has been a similar journey. I will probably never see God's purposes completely enough to make sense of why he allowed the events that led up to this addiction in the life of one of his own children. But I can choose to trust God's "bigger picture" and believe that he has my son's best interests in mind as well as the interests of everyone else. Only God can put all of the pieces together and have them make sense. I can't wait until we get to heaven and see all of God's purposes fulfilled! Until then, trusting God's purposes is a choice I want to keep working to make every time the enemy tempts me to doubt.

Think about the struggle you described at the beginning of this chapter. What have we talked about that could have helped you trust God's purposes better? _____

_____

_____

_____

_____

Lesson 7

Trusting God's Timing

Trusting God's purposes and trusting God's timing are closely related. If we believe God has a purpose in what we are going through, it's easier to wait for that purpose to be revealed. But humans live in a different world than God does. While he is *above* time, we are hopelessly stuck *in* time. Time determines our schedules, our activities, our eating, our sleeping, everything.

Many years ago, while attempting to lose a significant amount of weight, I learned a very important principle: eat when I'm hungry rather than when the clock says it's time to eat. But, even though this principle has served my body well, it isn't one that is culturally acceptable; and cultural norms serve as the gauge for productivity, success, and correct living. We're *supposed* to eat at certain times, sleep at certain times, work at certain times, and play at certain times. It doesn't matter that some people are hard-wired to be "night" people instead of "morning" people or that some are more productive at midnight than at 8:00 am. Society and culture determine our schedules and decide acceptable norms. Then our whole lives become an exercise in trying to fit into those norms and make time work for us instead of feeling driven by it.

Unfortunately, this perspective also affects how we approach God. We expect God to somehow fit into our time constraints instead of seeking to look at our lives from his eternal perspective. We try to apply human principles to God instead of applying God-principles to life on earth.

It seems to me that twenty-first century Americans particularly struggle with time. Unlike some of our predecessors who knew the value of waiting for hopes to be realized and dreams to be fulfilled, we live in a society of instant gratification. We want what we want when we want it—sooner, if possible! We have lost sight of patient endurance and perseverance in achieving goals, what Friedrich Nietzsche called a "long obedience in the same direction". We simply don't wait very well; in fact, we spend a lot of time trying to *avoid* waiting rather than embracing the process. We seek to master time and expect everyone else to do the same.

Several years ago, our family had an experience that helped us to recognize this cultural preoccupation with time. As four members of a group of fifteen people from our church who participated in a worship team mission trip to Honduras, we and the rest of our team took with us our North American mindset along with our voices and instruments. Our trip did not involve building a church or going door-to-door to spread the gospel. Our purpose involved presenting concerts in three major cities (along with a local Christian musician and an internationally-known Christian singer) as well as traveling to smaller churches in rural areas and joining with the local church in their weekly worship. We came to Honduras with a musical plan, having been encouraged by our American friend who lived and worked in the country that flexibility would be necessary; but it didn't take long to recognize what this would mean.

The day before our first concert, our expectation was this: we would arrive at the local church, set up our instruments, do a sound check, and be able to practice for a significant amount of time. We thought

72

we had prepared ourselves for flexibility, but we were still thinking like North Americans. The reality of that day included very little practice time and graciously being served a meal at the pastor's house. On the day of the concert, we waited over three hours for our ride to arrive and rushed to be ready for our performance. We began to understand a little about cultural differences. The next two weeks would offer many more opportunities for our perspective on time to change, and we are grateful to our Honduran brothers and sisters for helping us to grow in our understanding of the importance of relationships (as opposed to our focus on "the tyranny of the urgent"[1]). But it was not without some pain and anxiety that we learned to be more flexible.

One of the most important things we can do in our effort to trust God's timing is to recognize the difference between God's perspective and ours. The problem we have with that is what Ecclesiastes 3:11 tells us: "He has planted eternity in the human heart . . ." (NLT). So, while our hearts have God's perspective planted in them, our bodies are stuck in time, which causes us to be impatient. But this verse is actually encouraging to me because it reminds me that this is not my home! I'm not supposed to be completely satisfied with life here on earth because I was created for something different. I'm supposed to feel the ache of unmet expectations and shattered dreams because, along with everyone else, I'm waiting for my eternal home. In *The Sacred Echo*, Margaret Feinberg puts it this way: " . . . waiting is woven into the fabric of history. God is waiting. Creation is waiting. Humankind is waiting."[2] She goes on to point out that, although we humans think waiting is unbearable, God was actually the first being to ask the question, "How long?" (in Exodus 10:3 when he sent Moses and Aaron to Pharaoh). God's wait for all of humankind to repent and be restored to meaningful relationship with him must be excruciating, but we can learn something from *how* he waits. Second Peter 3:9 tells us about God's patience: "God isn't late . . . as some measure lateness. He is restraining himself . . ." (MSG). Because time is purely relative with God, he is able to wait patiently. The verse before this quotes an idea first penned in Psalm 90:4: "A day is like a

73

thousand years to the Lord, and a thousand years is like a day" (NLT). The idea from the Old Testament version of this is that, for God, a thousand years is like one night's sleep for us—a period of time where we are unaware of the passage of time. God does not view time as humans do, and he is completely unrestricted by time.

The Biblical writers and characters had their share of dealing with the disparity between God's perspective of time and ours, so they are a good resource for us in our efforts to trust God's timing. To name just a few: David was anointed as king at age sixteen but didn't actually take the throne until age thirty, Abraham and Sarah waited decades to have a child, and Habakkuk the prophet was told by God about the fall of Babylon and the end of Israel's captivity about sixty-six years before it actually came to pass. These are some examples of serious waiting! But look up these verses and write what David's wait taught him about perspective:

Psalm 39:4-5 _____

_____

Psalm 103:15 _____

_____

Psalm 144:4 _____

_____

As we face the struggle to understand God's timing throughout the circumstances of our lives, it is important for us to remember that our entire lifetime is just a moment to him. It is also helpful for us to have examples of others who waited on God's promises and to recognize that we are part of a whole human race that is waiting for things to be the way they were intended to be. But we still need the encouragement from Hosea 12:6: "Wait for your God, and don't give up on him—ever!" (MSG). This verse reminds us that God can be trusted beyond what we can see at any given moment in time. We can depend on him because he is eternal. When we are "in God's waiting room", we need to remember to trust God's heart and everything that we know about his character: his sovereignty, his wisdom, his justice, and his loving thoughts toward us (see previous chapters for help in these areas). When we forget to do this, we end up trying to tell God when the *right time* is and "how long" is too long. In other words, we try to control things that are not ours to control. We need the chiding Jesus' first disciples received when he was about to ascend to heaven: "You don't get to know the time. Timing is the Father's business" (Acts 1:7, MSG). And we need to remember that it is God who sets the timetable for all events—worldwide, national, and personal. God will act when he is ready and do what needs to be done, not necessarily what we would like him to do. We may not always *like* his timetable, but we definitely can *trust* it based on everything we know about him.

As a reminder, look up the following verses and write what they tell you about God's timing and his heart toward you:

Psalm 75:2 _____

_____

Isaiah 30:18 _____

_____

Isaiah 64:4 _____

_____

Now comes the tricky part. Once we accept that God's perspective of time is nothing like ours, that we cannot control all of the time-related issues in our lives, and that God can be trusted to have our best interests in mind when he asks us to wait, the next question becomes obvious: what do we DO while we are waiting? In many ways, how we answer this question is the most critical piece to the puzzle because this is often the only piece that we can actually control. Instead of trying to avoid or just endure waiting, we need to learn how to embrace and respond Biblically to waiting. The Biblical writers knew a lot more about waiting than we twenty-first century Americans do, so we need to listen to what they have to say on the subject.

Look up the following verses and identify both positive and negative ways of waiting on God:

Psalm 5:3 _____

_____

Psalm 27:14 _____

_____

Psalm 33:20 _____

_____

Psalm 37:7 _____

_____

Psalm 37:34 _____

_____

Psalm 130:5 _____

_____

Habakkuk 3:16 _____

_____

Romans 8:23-25 _____

_____

Galatians 6:9 _____

_____

Hebrews 6:12 _____

_____

James 5:7-8 _____

_____

In these few verses, I've identified at least thirteen different ways that we can respond when we are asked to wait—eight positive and five negative. While we are prone to become fearful, tired/weary, discouraged, indifferent or disinterested, and even lazy or spiritually dull, God's desire is that we learn to wait quietly, patiently, with hope, courage, expectancy, and confidence in him while continuing to depend on him and persevere/endure or stay on track. Each of these positive responses to God's timing are strong character traits; and, for God, the *process* of getting to where we (more often than not) exhibit these positive ways of waiting is the most important thing. He often uses times of waiting to refresh, renew, and teach us; we sometimes view times of waiting as proof that God isn't in control or is unfair. We think waiting means that God isn't answering or doesn't care about the urgency (as we perceive it) of our situation. Unlike the word picture of planting and harvesting we see in Galatians 6:9, we act like impatient children; and we lose hope along the way.

Hope plays a major role in our ability to wait properly, and once again the Biblical writers understood this better than we do. Most of us are familiar with Proverbs 13:12: "Hope deferred makes the heart sick . . ." (NLT, NIV); but we are largely unfamiliar with the kind of lengthy process of hoping that the Old Testament writers knew as they waited for their Messiah. They learned to put their hope in God's word (Psalm 130:5) as they waited; and, in Lamentations 3, we see that the same Hebrew phrase is translated both as "I have hope" (v.21, NIV) and "I will wait" (v. 24, NIV). Waiting involved hoping, and the Hebrews knew what verses 25 and 26 go on to say, "The LORD is *good* to those whose hope is in him . . . it is *good* to wait quietly for . . . the LORD" (NIV, emphasis mine). In the New Testament, Romans 8:25 reminds us again that hope really means waiting patiently. Unfortunately, this is not always what we do while waiting.

Margaret Feinberg's experience waiting for a spouse taught her some valuable lessons about God's timing. She describes how she "transitioned from actively living to passively waiting. My verve for life waned, subtly stripping life of its Technicolor."[3] She goes on to say that "waiting always leads to the same place: *In-between"*, a place where "you aren't fully here and you aren't fully there."[4] The reality of *In-between* is that it is "that place of blind trust where the precepts of faith meet the narrow path of fortitude, and movement is demanded though there's no definitive place to go but forward."[5] Feinberg reminds us that, when God's timing doesn't match ours, we must decide what we will do with the time. We can "dig in" or "pull back", and we face a "wrestling match . . . to be fully present, vested in the here and now, no matter what may come."[6] I can relate very well to what she is talking about.

When our first son was two years old, Ron and I began planning for the birth of a second child, which we hoped would occur soon after. As a fulltime, stay-at-home mom who found great joy and blessing from my role, I was very excited about pouring my life into another child. But, as we tried unsuccessfully for nearly two years and experienced all of the painful emotions and sometimes humbling procedures and questions surrounding infertility, my attitudes began to erode. I became bitter and angry at God, especially when others with less parenting desire were allowed to keep having unplanned or unwanted children. I not only questioned God's timing, but at times I also questioned his wisdom and his personal care for me. Our third bedroom was fully ready for a new baby—crib and all—and in many ways my life was on hold. While I still parented my little boy with love and joy, inside my heart was breaking. For most of this time of waiting, I was neither fully present nor vested in the here and now. Instead of actively living, I became passive, focused only on the waiting.

What we all need when we are faced with times of waiting on God is an eternal perspective: a glimpse of what God sees instead of only what we see. Paul recognized this in his second letter to the Corinthian church when he encouraged them to fix their gaze on things that cannot be seen because "the things we see now will soon be gone, but the things we cannot see will last forever" (2 Cor. 4:18, NLT). With the right perspective, we actually discover that the *benefits* of waiting far outweigh the *difficulty* of waiting. It's interesting to me that one of the first activities that the early church was asked by God to do was to wait (see Acts 1:4). I think that means we're on to something here! Unlike our natural way of thinking, waiting is a part of God's eternal plan and purpose in order to grow our character and prepare us for eternity. Feinberg says that "sometimes I think God loves the tension of *In-between* . . . the humility it creates within our hearts. The prayers that emerge from our spirits. The childlike cries from our innermost beings that acknowledge utmost dependence."[7] Growth. Character development. The key is to accept God's invitation to "place the weight of the wait on him. He does not want us to wait alone, but rather to wait on him alone."[8]

This is what we are promised in the well-known words of Isaiah 40:31: " . . . those who wait upon GOD get fresh strength. They spread their wings and soar like eagles, they run and don't get tired, they walk and don't lag behind" (MSG). One benefit of waiting on God is that we learn to exchange our strength for his like a change of clothes. This reminds me of the apostle Paul's encouragement for us to clothe ourselves with Christ (see Romans 13:14) and to put off the old sin nature and put on the new Christlike nature (see Ephesians 4:22 & 24). Trusting God's timing is just one way of appropriating what we have been given in Christ; in the process, we learn the importance of waiting for God's best and for the blessings that only come from waiting.

My struggle in God's waiting room of infertility brought blessings in my walk with God that I never could have imagined. I learned to trust God in a new way, and my heart was taught the importance of a willing spirit. Within two weeks of relinquishing my future to God and deciding to get on with my life as a mother of one, changing the nursery from a room-in-waiting to a spare room, I was pregnant with our second son! God's timing for our second son's birth had little to do with the things that I thought mattered and everything to do with growing my character in the process.

Do you have an experience of waiting on God where you clearly saw his purpose or perspective when all was said and done? _____

_____

_____

_____

If you still struggle to understand his timing in this experience, what have you learned so far in this lesson that might help you in the process? _____

_____

_____

_____

Sometimes we need to focus on what God *has* done in and through us rather than on what he has left *undone*. We also have to remember that what we are waiting for may not always come in this lifetime. My mother's uncle was a godly man whose children didn't follow his spiritual leading. He prayed consistently for them all of his life; however, it was his death that brought one of them back to the Lord. He didn't get to see the fulfillment of his waiting, but he will spend eternity with at least one of his children. From a prison cell near the end of his life, John the Baptist (Jesus' cousin and the one chosen to proclaim the Messiah's arrival a short time earlier) questioned whether Jesus was really "the one" because he was still waiting for Jesus to fulfill Isaiah's prophecy of freedom for the captives. This prophecy was accomplished on the cross, but it occurred after John's death. Trusting God's timing means we don't get lost in our *own* timetable but instead discover, accept, and appreciate God's *perfect* timetable. As the writer of Ecclesiastes teaches us: "There's an opportune time to do things, a right time for everything . . . God made everything beautiful in itself and in its time . . ." (Ecc. 3:1 & 11, MSG).

After our business closed, it became necessary for me to work outside the home for the first time in over twenty-three years. I hit the ground running, confident in my abilities and in this fact: in my previous working life, I had never failed to secure a job for which I had applied. When it took nearly six months to find someone who wanted to hire me, I experienced a downward spiral of emotions while waiting for God's best and trying to deal with everything else that had happened with our business and church. I am very grateful for Beth Moore's book *Get Out of That Pit* that I was reading at the time,[9] but mostly for the Scripture that the book is based on—Psalm 40:1-3:

> "I waited patiently for the LORD to help me, and he turned to me and heard my cry. He lifted me out of the pit of despair, out of the mud and the mire. He set my feet on solid ground and steadied me as I walked along. He has given me a new song to sing, a hymn of praise to our God. Many will see what he has done and be amazed. They will put their trust in the LORD." (NLT)

These verses have become "my verses" for the second half of my life on earth because they spoke directly to me at a time when I needed desperately to hear God's voice. As I waited on God (not always patiently!), I chose to believe what these verses said before I saw anything happening. Before I could feel God's help or hear any "new song" to sing, I believed that God would give it and that "many will see what he has done and be amazed". In the process of waiting, I experienced God lifting me out of the pit of despair, setting my feet on solid ground, and steadying me as I walked. I'm still experiencing the truths of these verses nearly five years later. I still sometimes feel the pain of waiting as described in *The Message* translation of verse 1: "I waited and waited and waited for GOD. *At last* he looked; *finally* he listened" (emphasis mine). I'm still figuring out everything that is involved in this new song I'm singing, which includes writing this book—another one of the pieces of God's timing that doesn't make sense to me. Why am I being directed by God to write a book NOW, when I'm working outside the home and have very little time to devote to it? I don't know the answer, except that the lack of answers makes me recognize more clearly my utter dependence on God for every step of the way. And, if God's timing always made sense to me, I wouldn't need to trust, which is what my relationship with God is all about. I don't know about you, but I can't wait for our home in eternity where time as we know it no longer exists! Until then, I choose to keep trusting God's timing no matter what it looks like from my perspective.

Describe a time where you experienced *In-between* as you waited for God's timing. How did you respond? What did you do right? What could you have done differently? _____

_____

_____

_____

_____

In thinking about your experiences in "God's waiting room", what do you think is your main obstacle to trusting God's timing? _____

_____

_____

_____

Is there one verse that you have read in this lesson that will be particularly helpful to you as you wrestle with God's timing in the future? _____

_____

_____

Lesson 8

Trusting God's Protection

The Bible makes it clear that God protects his people, and we often pray for him to keep us or our loved ones safe. But what does God's protection really mean, and what does it really look like? To be honest, what we want and what God gives is not always the same thing. Christians have tragic life-altering and painful accidents, and Christians die. Christians experience abuse as innocent children, and Christians can be deceived by Satan before they're old enough to recognize it. Even Christians in God's church can be mistreated and deceived by their own pastors or other leaders, resulting in an environment that is unsafe at best. What we want is pain-free living in a fallen, sinful world; what God promises is often quite different. How do we get to the point where we can reconcile the two and trust his protection in the way he intended us to?

As in previous chapters, what we discover when we discuss God's protection is that his perspective and our perspective are not the same. As self-centered humans who know only a small part of what the world is *really* about, our idea of what is good is very different from God's idea of what is good. God is looking at different things than we are when he promises to protect us; and he is looking for different purposes and goals or outcomes than we are when he protects us. As the Puritans recognized, God may allow one evil to touch our lives in order to shield us from greater evils.[1]

The two prayers that Jesus gave us during his time on earth help us to understand this better. When Jesus taught his disciples to pray in Matthew 6:9-13 (commonly known as *The Lord's Prayer*), he directed them to ask for deliverance from evil or the evil one (v. 13); and, when Jesus prayed for his disciples in the garden just before his arrest, he also asked God to protect them from the evil one (see John 17:11-12 & 15). He went on to include all future believers (that's us!) in this request. Notice that, in verse 15, he makes it pretty clear what he is NOT asking protection from: Jesus does not expect that we will be protected from the effects of living in a fallen world or that this life's inherent storms will never touch us.

The purpose or goal of God's protection for us is clear in these verses as well as in other passages: " . . . protect them . . . so that they will be united . . ." (John 17:11, NLT), and "For everything . . . is intended for his glory" (Romans 11:36, NLT). While we look at things from a limited perspective, God is interested in eternal things. His protection is designed to bring unity, to restore relationship and purpose to all of his creation, and to ultimately result in the coming of his eternal kingdom and the glory he deserves. These purposes are far greater than simply helping us to avoid pain, and they help us to understand what life has shown us: we do not have a guarantee that all believers will be protected from everything we would like to escape. Frankly, God owes nothing to any of us; and, while he deeply cares about what happens to us, his care includes an eternal perspective and purpose that we cannot fully comprehend this side of heaven. But stick with me: we're about to discover what God's protection REALLY means and how that affects our daily living.

Before we go there, however, it's important to look at the many different words the Biblical writers used to talk about God's protection because each word has a unique meaning and helps us get a better picture of what God does for us each day of our lives. I could probably come up with a whole book on this topic because there are so many words used: refuge, safety, shield, fortress, rock, stronghold, shelter, shadow, guard, horn, and portion (to name a few!); and we also discover that God not only rescues, shields, preserves, and fights the battle for us, but also that his name, his word, his mercy, his love and faithfulness, truth, a life of wisdom, and our faith all help to protect us. There's certainly a lot here to talk about, so let's start by looking up some verses and listing what words are used to describe God's protection.

2 Samuel 22:2-3 _____

Psalm 3:3 _____

Psalm 17:8 _____

Psalm 18:2 _____

Psalm 27:1 & 5 _____

Psalm 31:2-3 _____

Psalm 32:7 _____

Psalm 59:9 & 16-17 _____

Psalm 142:4-5 _____

Psalm 144:2 _____

Where do we start? Let's just reiterate a few of the recurring themes in these verses, using some of my favorite translations. "GOD is bedrock under my feet, the castle in which I live, my rescuing knight . . . my mountaintop refuge . . ." (2 Sam. 22:2-3, MSG); "Guard me as you would guard your own eyes. Hide me in the shadow of your wings" (Psalm 17:8, NLT); "The LORD is my rock, my fortress, and my deliverer . . . my shield and the horn of my salvation, my stronghold" (Psalm 18:2, NIV); "The LORD is the defense of my life . . . He will conceal me . . . He will hide me . . . He will lift me up . . ." (Psalm 27:1 & 5, NASB); "GOD's my island hideaway, keeps danger far from the shore . . ." (Psalm 32:7, MSG); " . . . you've been a safe place for me, a good place to hide" (Psalm 59:16, MSG); "He is my loving ally and my fortress, my tower of safety, my rescuer. He is my shield, and I take refuge in him" (Psalm 144:2, NLT). These phrases give us a good idea of what God's protection means, but the meanings behind the words provide us with a deeper understanding of what the Biblical writers were trying to convey.

Let's look again at Psalm 18:2, where several different words are used to describe God's protection. "Rock" is a common poetic figure for God and symbolizes his unfailing strength. A rock is something that can't be moved, so this is helpful in our picture of God's protection. A "fortress" is a place of safety where the enemy can't follow, and a "shield" is associated with victory and is positioned between us and harm. A "stronghold" is seen as a safe place that is high above our enemies, and "horn" symbolizes strength. As we see, God's protection is both practical and limitless, taking many different forms.

Psalm 17:8 provides us with a few other important word pictures. "Shadow" was a conventional Hebrew metaphor for protection against oppression (in the same way that "shade" protects from the oppressive heat of the hot desert sun). Kings were spoken of as the "shade" of those dependent on them for protection, so God is our protective shade. "Wings" is a metaphor for the protective outreach of God's power; so to be hidden in the shadow of his wings means that we are completely or fully covered by the shade of his protection just as baby birds are covered by their mother's wings. This verse also uses the phrase "the apple of your eye", which literally is "little man of his eye". It refers to the pupil, which is a delicate part of the eye that is essential for vision and therefore must be protected at all costs. God's protection of us involves guarding us as he would guard his own eyes.

In Psalm 142:4-5, David looks to his "right" and finds that no human is looking out for him. In Biblical times, a person's helper or defender was always standing at his right hand. David goes on to name God as his only refuge or "portion", a word which refers to someone who sustains or preserves life. So we see that God is our helper, defender, and sustainer who stands right next to us.

When I was studying for this lesson, the word "refuge" kept popping up. The Biblical writers used this word a lot to describe God's protection. I was reminded about the concept of *cities of refuge* presented in the Old Testament and decided that we probably needed to look at this in order to fully understand what the writers were referring to when they used the term "refuge". The cities of refuge are fully described in three different passages (see Numbers 35:9-15, Deuteronomy 19:1-10, and Joshua 20:1-6), and they were a provision that God made for the Israelites when they were settling the promised land of Canaan.

The cities of refuge were God's temporary solution to preventing injustice in an ancient culture that accepted and embraced revenge. They were a safeguard against miscarriage of justice for God's chosen people in a new land of pagan neighbors.

Basically, six cities were set aside as sanctuaries for *accidental* killers—a place of mercy and grace for those who didn't deserve punishment. Because the killer could be overtaken and killed (by the relatives of the deceased) on the road to the city of refuge, two students of the law were appointed to accompany the killer as he traveled. Not only that, but the roads to the cities of refuge were also to be kept in the best possible repair—all hills removed, every river bridged, and at least thirty-two cubits (about forty-eight feet) wide—to aid quick movement to the place of safety. There was even a sign posted at every turn so that no one could get lost along the way! As long as the killer stayed in the city of refuge, he was protected against revenge and possible injustice.[2]

The parallels to trusting God's protection are obvious. When the Old Testament writers spoke of God as our refuge, they had this picture in their minds. God protects us from injustice and protects those who cannot protect themselves, as we see in Psalm 116:6 ("GOD takes the side of the helpless . . .", MSG) and Isaiah 25:4 (" . . . a defense for the helpless, a defense for the needy in his distress, a refuge from the storm, a shade from the heat . . .", NASB). Since we could all be described as "helpless", this means God is a refuge for every one of us.

Beyond the variety of words we find in the Bible to describe God's protection, there are also specific things mentioned that protect us besides God himself: aspects of either his character or our walk with him that are worth noting. Look up the following verses and list what specific thing provides protection.

Psalm 40:11 _____

Psalm 61:7 _____

Proverbs 10:29 _____

Proverbs 14:26 _____

Proverbs 18:10 _____

1 Peter 1:5 _____

In these verses, we find that God's love, truth, and faithfulness protect us, as well as his mercy. When Proverbs 18:10 tells us that "the name of the LORD is a strong fortress" (NLT), we need to recognize that, in Old Testament culture, a person's name referred to his whole person. God's name has no separate existence apart from God himself and expresses all of his nature and qualities. To have God's name protecting us is to have all of God protecting us. These verses also show us *our* role in being protected. Just as the accidental killer had to run to the city of refuge, it is our fear of the Lord that is a tower of protection for our entire family ("He who fears the LORD has a secure fortress, and for his children it will be a refuge", Prov. 14:26, NIV). Similarly, a life of wisdom protects us ("The way of the LORD is a refuge for the righteous", Prov. 10:29, NIV). As we see in 1 Peter 1:5, our faith is one of the pieces God uses to complete the puzzle of his protection for us: " . . . through your faith, God is protecting you by his power . . ." (NLT). As with the chosen Israelites, God is ready to provide his protection to those who are willing to fully trust him. What we get is so much more than what we give.

So what *do* we get? What can we count on in terms of protection, and how is it sometimes different from what we want? As we navigate an unsafe world, what should we be focusing on that might change our perspective on God's protection?

To begin answering these questions, let's remember what Jesus prayed for us (see John 17:15) and how he taught us to pray (see Matthew 6:13): protection from *the evil one*. What did Jesus understand that we don't see while we live our lives on earth? What we discover as we look into Scripture more closely is that there is a completely different unseen world where a battle for our souls is constantly being waged between God and Satan, angels and demons. This is the world that Jesus wanted us protected from, and this is the world in which we can absolutely trust God to keep us safe. When we discover that the Biblical meaning of "safe" is "set on high", we begin to understand that God is an *eternal* refuge, a " . . . safe place to hide . . ." (Psalm 46:1, MSG) from the evil one and all of his unseen helpers. As Beth Moore has said, "The Lord lets no harm befall us in the world where the truest threats lie . . . God always protects his children . . . in the unseen realm where demons hiss and the gates of hell quake."[3]

Probably the best book ever written about this unseen battle is *The Screwtape Letters* by C.S. Lewis, which I highly recommend that all Christians read.[4] It is an eerie but eye-opening look at what is constantly going on behind the scenes in the spiritual realm, and it reminds us of the truth of 1 Peter 5:8: "Stay alert! Watch out for your great enemy, the devil. He prowls around like a roaring lion, looking for someone to devour" (NLT). Satan's whole agenda is to destroy God's children, and we need to recognize this and understand the seriousness of it. But, thankfully, you do not need to be afraid of the evil one, because God " . . . rides across the heavens to help you . . . the eternal God is your refuge, and his everlasting arms are under you" (Deuteronomy 33:26-27, NLT). As Psalm 34:7 tells us, "GOD's angel sets up a circle of protection around us . . ." (MSG), a word picture that is beautifully depicted in another book, *Cosmic*

Christmas, by Max Lucado.[5] This Christmas favorite helps us to think about the spiritual battle that might have taken place when Christ was born as a human baby and to understand the reality of what God does for us every day: he " . . . preserves the souls of His godly ones (and) delivers them . . ." (Psalm 97:10, NASB). Jesus told us that his sheep " . . . are protected from the Destroyer for good. No one can steal them from out of my hand. The Father . . . is so much greater than the Destroyer and Thief. No one could ever get them away from him" (John 10:28-29, MSG); and John reminds us later that " . . . God's son holds them securely, and the evil one cannot touch them" (1 John 5:18, NLT). Sometimes we tend to get caught up in expecting God's protection in this world (from *perceived* evil) and forget that he has already given the protection of our souls (from *real* evil). We forget how valuable we really are to him (see Luke 12:6-7 and its context).

For many years, one of my favorite passages of Scripture has been Romans 8. After the apostle Paul has described the new life that God has given us in Christ, he talks about how even Christians will continue to face trials and struggles in this world and how God takes each circumstance and works to bring good out of it for his children rather than just delivering or protecting us from all the bad. Instead of reinforcing our perception that suffering means God is not protecting us, Paul reminds us that God is watching out for us in ways we can't even imagine:

> "With God on our side like this, how can we lose? If God didn't hesitate to put everything on the line for us, embracing our condition and exposing himself to the worst by sending his own Son, is there anything else he wouldn't gladly and freely do for us? And who would dare tangle with God by messing with one of God's chosen? Who would dare even to point a finger? The One who died for us—who was raised to life for us!—is in the presence of God at this very moment sticking up for us. Do you think anyone is going to be able to drive a wedge

between us and Christ's love for us? There is no way! Not trouble, not hard times, not hatred, not hunger, not homelessness, not bullying threats, not backstabbing . . . none of this fazes us because Jesus loves us. I'm absolutely convinced that nothing—nothing living or dead, angelic or demons, today or tomorrow, high or low, thinkable or unthinkable—absolutely *nothing* can get between us and God's love because of the way that Jesus our Master has embraced us." (Romans 8:31-39, MSG)

The fact is this: God himself is on our side, and Jesus is sticking up for us in the Father's presence every day as Satan accuses us (see Revelation 12:10). Roy Lessin has said it this way: "God is for you, Jesus is with you, the Holy Spirit is in you, and all of heaven's angels are on your side."[6] We simply don't know or understand what God's protection means and what he does every day to protect us. Instead of hoping that God would keep us safe 100% of the time from the things we can see, we should be thinking about what would happen to us if God removed his constant and unseen protection from us. And we should focus on what the Bible clearly teaches that he has provided for all of us at all times in terms of protection: his *presence* in the midst of a dangerous world. Never underestimate the importance of "God with us" and the incredible gift that we have been given.

In the Old Testament world, the neighbors of the Israelites worshipped many different gods, trusting each one for different aspects of life's journey. The one thing that all of these gods had in common was that they were distant from humans; so the people kept statues and other manmade pieces to represent the gods and believed that these brought the presence of the gods and therefore their help. Into this atmosphere, the one true God introduced the concept of a god who is near to humans and whose help is always present. To represent this, he gave the traveling Israelites a tabernacle covered with the cloud of his presence that went with them on their way to the Promised Land (see Exodus 40:34-38). Many years later, the temple was built in Jerusalem, and God's presence once again was represented by the cloud that filled it (see 2 Chronicles 5:13-14).

This idea that God could actually dwell with man was unique to the Hebrew people and was fully realized for all mankind with the coming of God in the form of Jesus as a human baby to earth—Immanuel, "God with us". For all of us who live after Jesus' return to heaven, God has given the Holy Spirit as a representation that God is still with us. The presence of the Holy Spirit is our seal or protection until Christ returns again just as a seal on an ancient letter indicated ownership and protected its contents. When Pilate wanted to make sure Jesus' tomb was secure so that his disciples couldn't steal his body and fake his resurrection, the soldiers "went and made the tomb secure by putting a seal on the stone . . ." (Matthew 27:66, NIV). The presence of the Holy Spirit is our proof that our souls are secure—that we have the ultimate protection of God.

Just as it was for the Israelites, having God's presence with us every step of the way is an amazing thing. God doesn't remove the dangers of living in a fallen world, but he always offers his presence to protect his faithful followers from the unsafe conditions we live in. Over and over the Old Testament writers recognized this truth: "How great is the goodness you have stored up for those who fear you . . . you hide them in the shelter of your presence . . ." (Psalm 31:19-20, NLT); "God's eye is on those who respect him . . . he's ready to come to their rescue in bad times; in lean times he keeps body and soul together" (Psalm 33:18-19, MSG); "The LORD is a refuge for the oppressed, a stronghold in times of trouble . . . you, LORD, have never forsaken those who seek you" (Psalm 9:9-10, NIV); "The LORD says, 'I will rescue those who love me. I will protect those who trust in my name . . . I will be with them in trouble'" (Psalm 91:14-15, NLT); and "He's . . . a personal bodyguard to the candid and sincere. He keeps his eye on all who live honestly, and pays special attention to his loyally committed ones" (Proverbs 2:7-8, MSG).

To guard literally means to be present, and Psalm 121 is a beautiful picture of what that meant for the Israelites and what it means for us:

> "I look up to the mountains; does my strength come from mountains? No, my strength comes from GOD, who made heaven, and earth, and mountains.
>
> He won't let you stumble, your Guardian God won't fall asleep. Not on your life! Israel's Guardian will never doze or sleep.
>
> GOD's your Guardian, right at your side to protect you—shielding you from sunstroke, sheltering you from moonstroke.
>
> GOD guards you from every evil, he guards your very life. He guards you when you leave and when you return, he guards you now, he guards you always." (MSG)

To give you a little bit of context, this psalm is part of a group of psalms sung by the Israelites as they made their way from their homes in rural Israel to the temple in Jerusalem for one of the annual feasts of celebration. Along the way, there were many opportunities for trouble to overtake them, and they were keenly aware of their need for God's protection. To affirm as they walked along that their helper was the very Maker of Heaven and Earth meant that they had the best protector to trust. Because God created the world and it belongs to him, we can trust him to preserve and care for his creation. His perfection does not allow him to create and then forsake, for "all the earth's turf is God's turf. We will never go anywhere God has abandoned precisely because He will never abandon us."[7] The writer of this psalm affirmed what we all need to know: God provides unfailing protection against all that distresses or threatens, and nothing diverts or deters him. Because he never sleeps, he is in perfect attendance to every step we take whether in the day or at night. Nothing surprises him, and nothing distracts him. He is always present: "God with us". God's character trait of faithfulness is our assurance of protection, for " . . . the Master never lets us down. He'll stick by you and protect you from evil" (2 Thessalonians 3:3, MSG).

Think about a time when you knew without a shadow of doubt that God was present with you and write the specifics of what that felt like.

_____

_____

_____

_____

So what is the result of believing what God's Word says and trusting God's protection? How will our lives look different when we truly trust God to protect us? God is always present, but what do we need to do to appropriate his presence?

First of all, we have to choose to trust God to protect us—to place ourselves under his protective covering by choosing to live our lives for his glory and to rest in what he offers. As Psalm 91:1-2 reminds us, it is only "those who live in the shelter of the Most High" that will "find rest in the shadow of the Almighty"; and, only if we join the psalmist in declaring that "He *alone* is my refuge, my place of safety . . . I trust him" (NLT, emphasis mine), will we find him to be faithfully present for us. Trusting God *alone* is a difficult task in a world that gives us many options for protecting ourselves. We have to land somewhere between common sense (like locking the doors to our homes) and trusting God's protection so that we are free to live a full life without fear and full of gratitude, patience, and hope.

God calls us to live free and joyful lives and provides the protection we need to do just that. If our security comes from God, there are things that we don't have to worry about, giving us freedom in our relationships and a new outlook on life. His protection "makes us robust with life" (Psalm 41:2, MSG); and we discover that "he is my fortress, I will not be shaken" (Psalm 62:6, NIV), which means nothing can disturb my well-being or unsettle my security. We even discover that what others think of us doesn't really matter because we are protected from that as well: "The fear of human opinion disables; trusting in GOD protects you from that" (Proverbs 29:25, MSG)! "Because you've always stood up for me, I'm free to run and play. I hold on to you for dear life, and you hold me steady as a post" (Psalm 63:7-8, MSG). "The spacious, free life is from GOD; it's also protected and safe" (Psalm 37:39, MSG). Join me in pursuing the robust, spacious, and free life God intended for us by choosing to trust his presence and the protection he has provided for us against anything and everything that could *really* harm us (from his eternal and perfect perspective). This is a daily process that is worth our effort. To God be the glory!

Read John 17:11 and Romans 11:36 again. What are the two main purposes or goals behind God's protection of us? _____

_____

How do these differ from our motivation when we pray for protection?

_____

_____

_____

How can God's perspective help us when bad things happen to our loved ones? _____

_____

_____

_____

Which words of protection (used in the Old Testament verses we looked up) and their meanings are the most meaningful to you and why? _____

_____

_____

_____

Read Ephesians 6:10–18 and list the specific tools God has given us that provide protection from the evil one. _____

_____

_____

_____

In terms of protection, why is the gift of God's presence with us in this life so important? _____

_____

_____

_____

How can we trust his presence in our lives and the protection he provides for us? _____

_____

_____

_____

_____

Lesson 9

Trusting God Through Loss

Loss can come in many forms. Loss of life or a loved one; loss of a job; loss of a friendship or other relationship; loss of a home, a business, or other assets; loss of a ministry; loss of mental or physical abilities; loss of memory; loss of purpose; loss of innocence; loss of self-esteem: these are just a few. I want to begin this chapter by acknowledging that I have not experienced the untimely loss of immediate family or friends in a tragic accident, the miscarriage of a child, or other unexpected loss of life. While there is never a time that we welcome having to say goodbye to those we love, the losses of loved ones that I have experienced so far have been "expected" and "joyful" in the sense that my grandmothers, my father, and others in my extended family were elderly adults who had lived full and meaningful lives and who all passed from presence in this life to the presence of God in eternity.

All loss is painful, but it is particularly the *unexpected* losses that affect our ability to trust God. Often we question his sovereignty and thoughts toward us as well as his purposes and protection. I know from experiencing several different types of significant unexpected loss that trusting God is essential through the process of coping with any loss—and yet often the most difficult thing to do. All loss brings the same result to those affected: the experience of brokenness, emptiness, and feelings of hopelessness. In this atmosphere, trust is not a given. The challenge is to find a way to move from feeding the negative results of loss in our lives to focusing on the positive things God can do in us through the loss. As one of my good friends recently experienced when all of her children and grandchildren moved from living next door to her to living scattered across the country, this involves what Paul taught us in 2 Corinthians 10:5: " . . . we take captive every thought to make it obedient to Christ" (NIV).

So how do we turn the negative of loss to the positive of trust and growth? I believe the first step is to embrace the loss rather than deny it. The well-known words of Ecclesiastes 3:1-8 encourage this action:

> "There is a time for everything, and a season for every activity under heaven:
>
> a time to be born and a time to die,
> a time to plant and a time to uproot,
> a time to kill and a time to heal,
> a time to tear down and a time to build,
> a time to weep and a time to laugh,
> a time to mourn and a time to dance,
> a time to scatter stones and a time to gather them,
> a time to embrace and a time to refrain,
> a time to search and a time to give up,
> a time to keep and a time to throw away,
> a time to tear and a time to mend,
> a time to be silent and a time to speak,
> a time to love and a time to hate,
> a time for war and a time for peace." (NIV)

Clearly, there is a time for everything, including loss. Loss is part of the human experience, but we don't always approach it that way. Instead, we try to protect ourselves from loss and pain, which can cause us to begin to die spiritually and emotionally as our lives turn inward. As Jesus said in Mark 8:35-37, "Don't run from suffering; embrace it . . . what good would it do to get everything you want and lose you, the real you? What could you ever trade your soul for?" (MSG). A denial of loss and pain leads to a devaluation of the *experience*, which the Bible presents as valuable in itself. We are called to respond to loss as a reality and face it with faith so that the changes that occur in us result in growth.

You see, change is an inevitable result of loss, but growth is not. Because loss takes something away from us, it changes who we are. Loss makes it necessary for us to redefine "normal" and figure out who we are without whatever we lost. Things are never "the same" again, and the first step to growth is to acknowledge the change in us, which validates the *experience* and begins to allow it to be valuable for us. But we can still choose to dwell in the *experience* (producing negative results) or to move toward the growth God wants in us by learning how to move *beyond* the loss into a new (and changed) walk of faith.

Growing in our walk of faith through the experience of loss requires that we understand a proper Biblical perspective on both gains and losses. So let's start by looking up some verses and writing what the Bible encourages us to try and gain (or "harvest" or grow in) in this life:

Psalm 90:12 _____

Psalm 119:104 _____

Proverbs 3:13 _____

Proverbs 8:5 _____

Philippians 3:7-11 _____

We are encouraged to gain a heart of wisdom, understanding, and good judgment and to make knowing Christ our ultimate goal and concern. The apostle Paul believed that everything else we gain in this life is worthless and that what we seek to gain indicates the difference between being self-centered and being centered in Christ: " . . . everything I once thought I had going for me is insignificant—dog dung. I've dumped it all in the trash so that I could embrace Christ and be embraced by him" (Phil. 3:7-8, MSG). In another passage, Paul continues this godly perspective on loss and life on earth: "Alive, I'm Christ's messenger; dead, I'm his bounty. Life versus even more life! I can't lose" (Philippians 1:21, MSG).

We are not called to cling to this life or to gain earthly possessions; we are called to loss—to lose ourselves in order to gain Christ. The entire message of the book of Ecclesiastes is that everything we gain on earth is futile apart from God, the only thing that really matters. Jesus continued this theme when he said, "If you cling to your life, you will lose it; but if you give up your life for me, you will find it" (Matthew 10:39, NLT). He repeated this in another passage: "If you grasp and cling to life on your terms, you'll lose it, but if you let that life go, you'll get life on God's terms" (Luke 17:33, MSG).

Clinging to this life means trying to escape physical loss and feeding our self-centered determination to be in charge. It represents a materialistic and individualistic perspective on life instead of an eternal one. A proper eternal perspective recognizes that whatever we have on earth is temporary and that everything we gain on earth is a gift from God. In fact, all our earthly gains actually *belong* to God because everything belongs to God. An earthly perspective makes us act as if we have a "right" to the gains God has given us, which leads to our interpretation of losses as injustice or unfairness. This difference in perspective is critical because where it leads is the difference between hope and hopelessness. When we experience loss, either response is a possible outcome.

Loss of any kind leaves us feeling hopeless; that is our first and inevitable response. But having a proper perspective on gains and losses helps to move us from hopelessness to hope and is essential if we are going to grow in our trust of God through the loss. Of course, in order for this to happen, our hope must be placed in God alone. Thornton Wilder said that "hope is a projection of the imagination; so is despair. Despair all too readily embraces the ills it foresees; hope is an energy and arouses the mind to explore every possibility to combat them . . .";[1] and Eugene Peterson added to this by saying that hope in God is "imagination put in the harness of faith". Hope gives God "room to work out our salvation and develop our faith while we fix our attention on his ways of grace and resurrection".[2]

The Hebrew people of the Old Testament who made the journey from their homes to Jerusalem to celebrate the annual festivals of worship understood the role of hope and expressed it well in Psalm 130:

> "From the depths of despair, O LORD, I call for your help. Hear my cry, O Lord. Pay attention to my prayer. If you, GOD, kept records on wrongdoings, who would stand a chance? As it turns out, forgiveness is your habit, and that's why you're worshiped. I wait for the LORD, my soul waits, and in his word I put my hope. My soul waits for the Lord more than watchmen wait for the morning, more than watchmen wait for the morning. O Israel, put your hope in the LORD, for with the LORD is unfailing love and with him is full redemption. He himself will redeem Israel from all their sins." (NLT, MSG, and NIV)

Their hope as they walked along was in God alone, and they fully expected him to show up and meet them on their journey. They recognized how important it was to have God with them as they traveled, and they identified for us one of the most important gifts God gives us when we experience loss: his *presence*. As we discussed in a previous chapter, we cannot overestimate the importance of the presence of God with us throughout our lives on earth. When we experience loss, healing comes when we allow God's presence to fill the hole that is left in our lives by the loss. Admittedly, God's presence is intangible and sometimes hard to grasp. We have to choose to believe that God "will Himself perfect, confirm, strengthen and establish" us through our time of loss (see 1 Peter 5:10, NASB) and learn to relish what we have rather than resent what we're now missing: " . . . and be satisfied with your present [circumstances and with what you have]; for He (God) Himself has said, I will not in any way fail you *nor* leave you without support. [I will] not, [I will] not, [I will] not in any degree leave you helpless, *nor* forsake *nor* let [you] down, [relax My hold on you].—Assuredly not!" (Hebrews 13:5, AMP). We have to choose to believe Psalm 29:11: "The Lord gives strength to his people; the Lord blesses his people with peace" (NIV).

When it became necessary for us to close our business and we were experiencing the hopeless feeling of loss that resulted from that decision, I stumbled upon a passage in a little-read book of the Old Testament that spoke to my heart in that situation:

> "Even though the fig trees have no blossoms, and there are no grapes on the vines; even though the olive crop fails, and the fields lie empty and barren; even though the flocks die in the fields, and the cattle barns are empty, yet I will rejoice in the LORD! I will be joyful in the God of my salvation! The Sovereign LORD is my strength! He makes me as surefooted as a deer, able to tread upon the heights." Habakkuk 3:17-19, NLT

Through these verses, God reminded me that, no matter what we have lost, we always have a choice how we respond. We can choose to focus on the loss, or we can choose to praise God in spite of the loss. We can let our feelings be controlled by what has happened to us, or we can let faith in God override our natural inclination to negative thinking. By fixing our eyes on God instead of the loss, we are able to make the choice to praise regardless of what has happened to us. Years later, the loss still hurts; but I can continue to choose praise and trust over the alternative thought patterns and live each day victoriously instead of allowing the enemy a foothold.

When we choose to trust God's presence in our lives and rely on him to take the place of what we lost, we receive another gift from him: the gift of contentment. The question that we all must face in our walk of faith is this: is God enough? If everything else is taken away, is God enough? Loss forces us to answer that question.

The apostle Paul was a content person despite the fact that he had no earthly possessions to speak of and no immediate family that we know of. He had also lost everything from his past that had meant anything to him (his standing in the Jewish community, his purpose in persecuting Christians, all of his previous friendships, etc.). Yet, out of this position of "lack", he penned two important passages on this topic. In 1 Timothy 6:6-8, he reminds Timothy to honor God by centering his desires on him alone and by being content with what God is doing in his life: " . . . godliness with contentment is great gain. For we brought nothing into the world, and we can take nothing out of it. But if we have food and clothing, we will be content with that" (NIV). Paul personalizes this idea in Philippians 4:11-13: " . . . I have learned to be content whatever the circumstances . . . I have learned the secret of being content in any and every situation . . . I can do everything through him who gives me strength" (NIV). Paul had learned through pain and loss to focus on what he was supposed to *do* rather than what he felt he should *have* and to trust God's promises and God's strength to bring contentment and accomplish his purposes and will.

But, even with God's gift of contentment, the pain from the loss never goes completely away. This is where we learn to trust another gift from God: redemption. Look up these verses and write who is included in God's redemption:

Psalm 34:22 _____

_____

Psalm 130:7 _____

_____

These verses tell us that those who serve God, those who place their hope in him, will receive redemption. But what does that mean? The Hebrews who wrote these Psalms fully understood the concept, but the idea of redemption escapes a nation that was founded and operates on freedom. The Israelites knew that they had to be redeemed (literally "delivered") because that is what God had done for them when they escaped from Egypt; but we Americans struggle to fully understand the meaning and therefore to fully experience what God offers.

According to Beth Moore, the Hebrew word for redemption used in Psalm 130, "padhah", includes much more than just redemption from sin: "Full redemption happens when God buys up or back everything that has happened to us . . ."[3] God can be counted on to redeem the loss we are experiencing, though it's hard to fully understand what that means. We don't get back what was lost exactly the way it was or would be if we hadn't lost it. Children who have been abused and lost their innocence while very young don't ever get it back. The Bible even tells us that Christ will bear the scars on his body for eternity to remind all of us what his redemption for sin really meant. Our experiences with loss and God's redemption carry this truth: while the wound may heal, the scar remains.

This is where trust in God's full redemption must be exercised. As Eugene Peterson points out in *A Long Obedience in the Same Direction*, we have to remember that God is at the foundation and the boundaries of all suffering and that whatever we are going through is not the bottom line and can never be ultimate. " . . . (O)ur place in the depths is not out of bounds from God . . . God's way with us is redemption and . . . redemption, not the suffering, is ultimate. The 'bottom' has a bottom . . ."[4] How God redeems doesn't have a single face because our losses are not all the same. Trusting God's redemption means that we believe in God's ability and desire to continue to work his good in us, regardless of our loss, and to use us in the future we have left after the loss.

You see, the brokenness we experience from loss is only negative to us, not to God. Often our usefulness to God after loss is not *in spite of* the loss but actually *because of* the loss. God's redemption means that "he not only diffuses our past of all power to harm and haunt us but He *infuses* it with power to help others. Redemption is incomplete if our negative past is only diffused . . . God won't get all the glory until the bad is used for good."[5] Matthew 16:25-26 reminds us that, if we try to protect ourselves from loss, we run the risk of losing our intended purpose. A better choice would be to allow God to use our losses to grow us and speak into the lives of those around us. Returning to Philippians 3:7-11, we see that the kind of knowledge that Paul wants is the knowledge that is gained through experience with God, which includes the experience of loss. This is the kind of knowledge that can transform our entire person and make us useful to God after the loss—when we feel utterly useless and Satan has convinced us that we have a corner on the market of pain. I am still overwhelmed at times by the thought of all that we have lost. But the world is full of people in pain because of loss, and God wants to use each and every one of us to minister to the needs of others and to model faith and trust to each other for our growth and for his glory. Let's agree to trust God through our losses and not allow them to have the final word.

What losses have you experienced so far in your life here on earth?

_____

_____

Describe your journey through your most difficult loss and the emotions you felt or still feel. _____

_____

_____

_____

_____

Reread Matthew 10:39 and Luke 17:33. In what ways do you try to "cling to your life", and in what ways could you choose more actively to "lose your life"? _____

_____

_____

_____

_____

Read Luke 14:33 and reread Philippians 3:7-11 (in several versions of the Bible, if available). How can Christ's words and Paul's perspective on gains and losses help you when you are facing loss?_____

_____

_____

_____

_____

How does knowing Christ better help you face loss differently? ___

_____

_____

_____

_____

Think again about your most difficult loss so far. How could an understanding of the gift of God's presence have affected (or still affect) your journey in a positive way? _____

_____

_____

_____

What experiences do you have with God filling the hole left by what you lost? _____

_____

_____

_____

How can you choose praise and contentment over bitterness and unrest? _____

_____

_____

_____

What experience do you have with God's "full redemption" in loss?

_____

_____

_____

_____

What is still left to be redeemed from your experiences of loss? What role does hope and your faith play in this process? _____

_____

_____

_____

_____

How can God use (or how has God already used) your most difficult loss to minister to the needs of others for their growth and his glory? What needs to change in your approach to loss in order for that to happen? _____

_____

_____

_____

Lesson 10

Trusting God Through Changes

Loss and change are closely related. All loss involves change of some kind, but not all changes involve loss. Good things like getting married and having children bring change to our lives even though they do not result from loss. The absence of loss, however, doesn't take away our need to trust God through the changes that we experience; but it can keep us from recognizing this need because the change doesn't seem to affect us in a negative way.

For some people, this chapter may seem unnecessary. Different personalities respond differently to change: some welcome it, while others loathe it. I fall into the second category; I like sameness, predictability, security. When my brother and I were younger, he used to chide me with the phrase "no pain, no gain" because I was content to water-ski on two skis and never fall rather than accept the challenge (and imminent failure before success) of learning to slalom ski like him. If you visit my house, you will see the same pictures on the same walls forever, and the furniture stays put as well. My hairstyle stays the same for years at a time. My motto is, "If it ain't broke, don't fix it." "Adventurous" is not a word that would be used to describe me!

With my personality, I would have been happy if my husband had stayed in the same job all of his working life and if we had lived in the same house most of our lives together as well. Seeing through the fallacies of my basic bent (in terms of spiritual growth), God has ordained that my husband has in fact worked for over ten different companies and we have moved into seven different residences since our first apartment over thirty years ago! Sometimes there has been a level of excitement connected with these changes (needing more space because of a new baby, etc.), but most of the time these changes have been difficult.

What makes change difficult? For me, there are several reasons why change is hard. First of all, change moves us out of our comfort zone, and newness can be scary. Change causes us to lose control of our own lives for a time, and none of us likes to feel out of control. We aren't sure where we stand or how we fit anymore, and we have to make adjustments in order to figure it out. Even God-ordained change requires adjustments despite our best intentions to seek God's will and follow it. When our older son got married a couple of years ago, our relationship necessarily changed. Even though this is the way it's supposed to be, and even though our daughter-in-law is a wonderful new part of our family, things are not "the same" as before they were married. We are still learning to adjust our approach as parents to this God-blessed change in our family just as we had to adjust to the changes in our children as they grew from being little boys in our home to young adults living away at college most of the time. Such is the nature of change.

Change also brings with it the loss of predictability and a lack of security. We lose the ability to have something we can "count on". We have to recognize that the things we counted on have become temporary, and we long for something permanent to even out the feeling of unrest that occurs in us. This is where it becomes important for us to place our trust in God and to find our security in his unchanging qualities instead of looking at our changing lives here on earth for answers. A thesaurus tells us that the opposite of change is constancy, consistency, and permanence. Only God perfectly possesses these qualities; so trusting him alone through our experiences with change seems like a productive choice to make. Let's look deeper at what the Bible tells us we can count on.

Look up the following verses and write what qualities of God we can depend on:

Numbers 23:19 _____

_____

Psalm 102:25-28 _____

_____

Psalm 146:5-6 _____

_____

Malachi 3:6 _____

_____

Hebrews 1:10-12 _____

_____

Hebrews 7:21 _____

_____

Hebrews 13:8 _____

_____

James 1:17 _____

_____

Here is what we know even if everything around us is changing: God always tells the truth and never changes his mind, always follows through on what he says and keeps his promises (Numbers 23:19). He is more enduring than what he has created; and because he doesn't change, the future of his people is secure (Psalm 102:25-28 and Hebrews 1:10-12). God "remains faithful forever" (Psalm 146:6, NIV): our hope during times of change is in a faithful God. We stand on the firmest foundation in the universe—our only security in a changing world. The personal name for himself that God gave to the Israelites, I AM, is used in Malachi 3:6 to help them understand his presence with them through all of the changes they experienced during their captivity in Babylon and their return to Judah: "I am GOD—yes, I AM. I haven't changed" (MSG). Though everything else might be in question, God's faithfulness and constancy are not. "God gave his word; he won't take it back" (Hebrews 7:21, MSG).

In our post-modern, ever-changing world, we discover that "Jesus doesn't change—yesterday, today, tomorrow, he's always totally himself" (Hebrews 13:8, MSG). And we are also told that God the Father "does not change like shifting shadows" (James 1:17, NIV), or, in another translation, " . . . with (him) there is no variation, or shadow of turning" (NASB). It's important that we focus on God's unchanging nature and learn to trust these qualities instead of our experiences. The twenty-first century world we live in doesn't offer my sons' generation the same thing it offered my father's generation: the stability and security of working at the same company for all of their forty to fifty-year careers. And the by-products of this instability are other changes—in housing, in church life, in friendships, and sometimes in the necessity (and not just the luxury) of two-income families. Aren't you glad that we have SOMETHING that is rock-solid and unchanging that we can depend on through all of life's changes? And aren't you glad that the something is a SOMEONE?

You see, in life, change is inevitable; and change is also part of the life of faith. "The life of faith has to do with extraordinary experience; the life of faith has to do with ordinary experience. Neither cancels out the other; neither takes precedence over the other . . . the life of faith has to do with the glories of discovering far more in life than we ever dreamed of; the life of faith has to do with doggedly putting one flat foot in front of the other, wondering what the point of it all is. Neither cancels out the other; neither takes precedence over the other.''[1] In the life of faith, both sameness and change can be God-ordained. Ecclesiastes 7:14 encourages us to "remember that nothing is certain in this life" (NLT). We can't predict the future or depend on human wisdom or power, and change keeps us from taking anything for granted. The only thing we can depend on in the midst of change is that God is in control and that, as we have seen in previous lessons, he is always working in every situation for our growth and his glory.

Change is not only a *part* of the life of faith, but the Bible also testifies to another truth: we are actually *called* to change. God's people have never been called to be the same as those around them—all the way from God's request for Noah to build an ark up until the New Testament times that we live in. The Israelite people were told to "be separate" (or different) from their non-Hebrew neighbors, and the life of faith has always been characterized by change and looking ahead or beyond the present. Jesus told his listeners in Matthew 18:3 that, "unless you *change* and become like little children" (NIV, emphasis mine), they could have no part in the Kingdom of Heaven. The apostle Paul continued this theme in Romans 12:2 when he told us to "let God transform you into a new person by *changing* the way you think" (NLT, emphasis mine). The kind of change that we are called to involves allowing the Holy Spirit to renew, re-educate, and redirect our thinking so that the result is a transformation into Christlikeness. This is not something we can do for ourselves, and it is a gradual, progressive process that will last for all of our lives here on earth: "And all of us . . . are constantly being transfigured into His *very own* image . . ." (2 Corinthians 3:18, AMP). We will never reach a point in this life where this call to change will diminish or be completed. From God's perspective, change is not only inevitable, but also preferable.

With this idea of spiritual change in mind, I looked up the word "change" in a thesaurus. These are a few of the more interesting words used as synonyms for change: reconstruction, reworking, regeneration, metamorphosis, remodeling, rearrangement, renewal, realignment, redirection, refinement, growth, transformation, revision, development. To be "different" means to be distinct, contrasted, contradictory, disparate, abnormal, startling, or jarring. And to be the "same" is described as identical, alike, or just-as-good. It's no wonder that change can be disturbing to us or that we sometimes respond the way we do to change. We want the newness brought about by change to feel *just-as-good* as everything was before the change. But recognizing that God calls us to change can make a difference in how we approach the seemingly non-spiritual changes in our lives as well.

If we are trusting in God's unchanging character and his purposes, we should find it easier to trust the process of change that is occurring throughout our lives on earth. Our spiritual, physical, and emotional lives are all inter-connected; this is part of the way God created us. Because of this, sometimes God ordains physical or emotional changes, as well as lifestyle changes, in order to effect the *spiritual* changes he wants in us. Many times we seek to control the changes by manipulating our circumstances rather than trusting God's work in us and walking by faith. We have to be willing to trust him enough to trust the process rather than getting sidetracked by the individual changes as they occur.

It is interesting to me to notice what 1 Corinthians 15:51–53 says about the end of this process of spiritual growth that we are all in the middle of: " . . . we are all going to be *changed* . . . we'll all be *changed* . . . everything perishable taken off the shelves and *replaced* by the imperishable, this mortal *replaced* by the immortal" (MSG, emphasis mine). Not only is this earthly life full of changes, but our first step into eternity will also involve change!

Which brings us to another important truth that we need to focus on when change comes our way: this world is not our home. In describing Abraham's faith, the writer of Hebrews says "he was waiting expectantly *and* confidently, looking forward to the city which has fixed *and* firm foundations, whose Architect *and* Builder is God" (Hebrews 11:10, AMP). Abraham was called by God to leave his secure and familiar surroundings and live in tents in a foreign land so that he could become the father of God's chosen people and ultimately all believers; but Abraham followed God's call in faith because his sights were set on the permanence of his eternal home rather than the difficult changes he was called to make here on earth.

Hebrews 13:14 reminds us that "this world is not our permanent home; we are looking forward to a home yet to come" (NLT). Like Abraham, our eyes need to be focused on what God is building in eternity, remembering that all that we are and have here on earth is temporary. In a world of constant changes, Christians need to be characterized by looking ahead instead of focusing on the present and being attached to this world. Then those around us will be able to see our faith and that we trust God through every change.

Following Abraham's example involves embracing change and approaching it with hope ("waiting expectantly and confidently"). Trusting God through changes means believing that what we *can't* see could be better than what we *can* see, which is the essence of properly placed hope. Sometimes this is easier to do than other times. Although I found it relatively easy to embrace the changes brought about by our encounters with cancer, diabetes, and heart disease, I experienced difficulty at the beginning of our newly changed lives after leaving our long-time church, losing most of our friendships, and having no regular ministry after over twenty-five years of continuous service. I kept waiting for life to feel the same as it used to as evidence that God was working, but this never happened. I thought I would just get past everything and be used by God again on the other side. It took some time to recognize God's desire and plan to actually use the *changes* themselves and the *process* for his glory.

So what are the results of trusting God through changes? Jesus taught us the value of having our security placed properly: "Stockpile treasure in heaven, where it's safe from moth and rust and burglars. It's obvious, isn't it? The place where your treasure is, is the place you will most want to be, and end up being" (Matthew 6:19-21, MSG). Earthly treasures will be destroyed, but eternal ones will last forever. Placing our trust in the security that God gives instead of the false securities of this world allows us to be a part of fulfilling his purposes in all that we do. This is more important than having a change-free life that we can control and manipulate for our own purposes.

Trusting God through changes also brings peace and contentment into our lives. We are all familiar with the words of Isaiah 26:3-4: "You will keep in perfect peace all who trust in you, all whose thoughts are fixed on you! . . . the LORD GOD is the eternal Rock" (NLT). But listen to another version of these verses: "People with their minds set on you, you keep completely *whole* . . . Depend on GOD . . . in the LORD GOD you have a *sure thing*" (MSG, emphasis mine). Peace and contentment come because we are supported by God's *unchanging* love and power—not our own—and, therefore, change is not able to shake us. We look to God to provide our contentment and security and discover that we are *whole* because we have a *sure thing* regardless of what is going on around us or happening to us. This is truly a peace that "transcends all understanding" (see Philippians 4:7, NIV) and is "a gift the world cannot give" (see John 14:27, NLT). I want to choose trust and a proper focus when faced with change so that the gifts of peace and contentment characterize my life on earth, my "home away from home".

> "I will bless the Lord forever. I will trust Him at all times.
> He has delivered me from all fear.
> He has set my feet upon a rock, and I will not be moved."[2]

What significant changes have you faced in your life so far? Which were the most difficult for you and why? _____

_____

_____

_____

In light of change, which of the verses we looked up at the beginning of this lesson are the most meaningful to you and why? _____

_____

_____

_____

How do God's unchanging qualities differ from your experiences in life so far? How could trusting in these qualities affect your experiences with change in the future? _____

_____

_____

_____

Read Romans 12:2 and 2 Corinthians 3:18. How do you feel about God's call on us to change, and how does accepting this call affect your approach to the changes life brings? _____

_____

_____

_____

_____

Read Hebrews 11:8-10. What can you learn from Abraham's example regarding our focus while we live on earth and the role of obedient trust when you are faced with change? _____

_____

_____

_____

How can a firm belief that "this world is not your home" affect how you respond to life's inevitable changes? _____

_____

_____

_____

Have you experienced the positive results of trusting God through change? Describe your experiences (or lack of experience) with God's peace and contentment amidst change. What kept you (or could have kept you) from being shaken or "moved"? _____

_____

_____

_____

_____

_____

Lesson 11

Trusting God's Silence

"Belief in God does not exempt us from feelings of abandonment by God."[1] "While many sounds can hurt our ears . . . silence is the most painful because it can hurt our hearts."[2]

We are afraid of silence. When we meet someone new in a social setting, silence is awkward and difficult. If our friends or loved ones don't respond to us with words, we assume the worst. And we have been led to believe that, if we experience the silence of God, there is something wrong with *us*.

But "any understanding of God that doesn't take into account God's silence is a half truth—in effect, a cruel distortion."[3] Speaking about God's deliverance of the Israelites after four hundred long years of Egyptian bondage, Eugene Peterson reminds us that God's silence is real: "The story in which God does his saving work arises among a people whose primary experience of God is his absence . . . this seemingly unending stretch of the experience of the absence of God is reproduced in most of our lives, and most of us don't know what to make of it. We need this Exodus validation that a sense of the absence of God is part of the story, and that it is neither exceptional nor preventable nor a judgment on the way we are living our lives."[4]

Other stories and passages in the Bible confirm the truth that God's silence is a real experience and one that is not always the result of our sin. Ecclesiastes 3:7 tells us that there is a *divinely appointed* "time to be silent and a time to speak" (NIV). In Job 23:8-9, we see that, no matter where Job looked, he couldn't find God; and, in Job 30:20, Job says that, despite his attempts to approach God, he got "nothing, no answer . . . you give me a blank stare!" (MSG). And Lamentations 3:44 clearly places the "blame" on God: "You have hidden yourself in a cloud so our prayers cannot reach you" (NLT).

The Psalms are full of cries for help from God in an atmosphere of experiencing God's silence. These verses not only voice our own experiences with God's silence, but they bring validation as well. Perhaps the best-known passage is the one that Jesus quoted when he was on the cross (see Matthew 27:46 and Mark 15:34):

> "God, God . . . my God! Why did you dump me miles from nowhere? Doubled up with pain, I call to God all the day long. No answer. Nothing. I keep at it all night, tossing and turning" (Psalm 22:1-2, MSG).

Other versions of these verses use the words "abandoned" (NLT) and "forsaken" (NIV). We can be encouraged to know that even Jesus deeply felt God's abandonment of him. Since Jesus was without sin, we know that his cry on the cross was not a cry of doubt but rather an expression of the reality of his experience of spiritual separation from God. God's silence was and is a real experience, and the first step toward trusting God's silence is to accept that it is real.

In his excellent book, *God On Mute,* Pete Greig uses the example of Passion Week to help us better understand the silence of God, indicating that "from dusk on Good Friday to dawn on Easter Sunday, God allowed the whole of creation to remain in a state of chaos and despair."[5] He says that the silence of God that we experience is "both epitomized and legitimized by the silence of God on Holy Saturday."[6] Although it *appeared* on Saturday that Satan had won and that God wasn't active, the *reality* was something quite different. When we are faced with God's silence, we need to remember this: just because God "sometimes withdraws from our conscious experience by deliberately making Himself less obvious and less immediately available"[7] doesn't mean that he has become inactive in our lives. In fact, during the two weeks that immediately preceded the beginning of the writing of this book, I experienced one of my most desperate times of God's silence!

So why is God sometimes silent? There are many answers to that question, and we will never know all of them. As Isaiah 59:1-2 indicated about the Israelites, our sin certainly plays a role in God's ability to speak to us: "The LORD's arm is not too weak to save you, nor is his ear too deaf to hear you call. It's your sins that have cut you off from God. Because of your sins, he has turned away and will not listen anymore" (NLT). Sin is also what caused Jesus' experience with God's silence on the cross—not his own sin, but the fact that he was carrying all of our sin, which made it impossible for God the Father to have a relationship with the Son at that point in time. But, just as Israel experienced reconciliation with God and a continuation of his voice speaking to them (see Isaiah 54:7-8), Jesus' relationship with God the Father was restored after the penalty for sin had been paid. The same is true for us: sin can separate us from God; but it is not the only reason that God's silence is a reality.

As we have seen before, one of the reasons for the ways God works in the world is to bring proper glory to himself and cause us to recognize his greatness and power. When Job asked for answers, the only one he got was for God to reveal his own greatness and power as the only answer Job needed. Sometimes God's silence isn't about us as much as it is about him. Remembering what we know to be true about God and trusting those things helps us to look past the silence we are experiencing and regain a proper perspective on the God of the universe, who has no obligation but still sometimes chooses to speak to those he has created.

This leads us to another important reason for God's silence: his commitment to our growth and maturity. In other words, God's silence is intentional and has a distinct purpose. As Greig says, "God has switched off for a while our ability to be conscious of His presence . . . in order to reduce our dependency on outward things . . .";[8] and, "until . . . we are left to stand alone without any reason for continuing except steadfast loyalty, we cannot truly mature from an us-centered relationship with God to a truly Christ-centered one. It isn't until the facts that once reinforced our beliefs are removed from our lives that we can truly 'live by faith and not by sight' (2 Cor. 5:7)."[9] We should not try to rush through the experience of God's silence and thereby avoid the value it has in our Christian walk. Sometimes the silence of God is what properly prepares us for future service for him.

Before that can happen, however, we have to get past the wrong assumptions that we are prone to make when God chooses to be silent.

Look up the following verses and look for key words that indicate what we assume about God when he is silent:

Psalm 22:1 _____

_____

Psalm 28:1 _____

_____

Psalm 38:21 _____

_____

Psalm 55:1 _____

_____

Psalm 77:7-9 _____

_____

Psalm 83:1 _____

Psalm 94:9 _____

The Hebrew word *harash* that is sometimes used for the silence of God means "the state of being dumb" and is usually combined with deaf.[10] The assumption is this: if God doesn't speak, he also doesn't hear. As the Psalm writers wrote in these verses, when God is silent for any length of time, we wonder whether he is deaf and assume that he doesn't care about us. Sometimes we wonder if he's really there at all. We interpret his silence as an indication that he is inactive or even that perhaps he lacks the power to help us. But, when Jesus was silent before the high priest Caiaphas prior to his crucifixion, he proved to us that silence does not necessarily mean a lack of power (see Matthew 26:63 and Mark 14:61); and we certainly know now that God's silence while Jesus was in the grave was not inactivity.

Whenever we begin to entertain any of these ideas about God while waiting for God to speak to us, we tend to fill in the blanks ourselves with other ideas or agreements that are not founded in truth—things like "God is not good", "God is not trustworthy", or "God does not care".[11] We decide how God should speak, when he should speak, and the circumstances under which he should speak. Then we make a decision about what his silence means, and our faith wavers as a result.

It's important to remember that God doesn't always speak to us in the way that we expect or in a way that we recognize as his voice; and, as we talked about in a previous chapter, his timing doesn't always match ours either. In Isaiah 54:7, God admits that he had abandoned Israel, but only "for a brief moment" (NLT); however, God's brief moment lasted for about fifty years of Babylonian exile! Sometimes we decide what God's voice should sound like, and we interpret everything else as God's silence; but God is not limited by our expectations or perceptions, and he rarely performs in the ways that we are accustomed to in this world. God speaks to us in various ways: through his creation, through his Word, through other people, through music, and often with a voice more like a whisper than a roar. As the prophet Elijah discovered in 1 Kings 19:11-13, God didn't speak in a big and powerful way—in the wind, the earthquake, or the fire—but in a gentle and quiet whisper. In order to hear God's voice, Elijah had to be quiet and humble enough to listen intently; and so do we.

My most difficult and longest continuous experience with God's silence came on the heels of closing our business and asking God for future direction, and it lasted for many months. This was undoubtedly the worst experience of my Christian walk so far, and the silence at times was deafening. I continued to seek God in all of the ways that had worked in the past, but he didn't seem to be available. He simply did not respond to me in any way that I could feel or grasp. When he finally decided to speak, it was extremely profound; he simply reminded me through two passages in his Word that I could trust his presence in my life:

> "Be strong and courageous! Do not be afraid or discouraged. For the LORD your God is with you wherever you go." (Joshua 1:9, NLT)

> "GOD is striding ahead of you. He's right there with you. He won't let you down; he won't leave you. Don't be intimidated. Don't worry." (Deuteronomy 31:8, MSG)

God didn't give me answers to the questions I was asking; he gave me himself. More than solutions to the problems that plagued me at the time, I needed to be reminded that God was with me—that he had always been there and would never leave, regardless of what my future looked like. Despite what I could *feel,* God was with me then as much as he ever had been. Whether I could hear his voice or not, he was still deeply involved in my life. The reality of "God with us"—not a feeling or a theory, but a physical reality—is that "when we are present in a situation . . . He cannot be absent."[12] *God with us* is a promise he has agreed to keep.

My experience reminds me of two other experiences described in the Bible that illustrate this truth. When Job had lost everything in his life and was devastated by the loss, three of his friends traveled to be with him and console him. But the first thing that they did was profound: they didn't speak a word for seven days and nights—they simply sat on the ground with him in silence (see Job 2:11-13). Although they loved their friend deeply, they discerned that what he needed right then was their companionship rather than their words. In the same way, we can count on God to always sit with us even though he may not always speak. His silence is sometimes the best way to convey his loving companionship to us.

The second story in the Bible that shows us God's commitment to be present with us is in 1 Kings 19. Elijah had reached the end of his rope. He was exhausted physically and had lost all hope spiritually. He felt completely alone and just wanted to die. At just the right moment, God spoke life and hope into his situation by sending a new prophet (Elisha) to be trained by Elijah to take over his work and to be with him as his assistant until God took Elijah home to heaven. This action countered Elijah's loneliness and despair with the assurance that he was not alone. God was with him, and so would Elisha be—even if everyone else was against him. God didn't fix all of Elijah's complaints, but instead he offered his presence and a human companion to journey with him and carry on his ministry.

In *The Sacred Echo*, Margaret Feinberg describes her own experience with the reality of God's presence during her struggle with a difficult physical illness. As she begged God for answers, she got no reply: only silence. Then she became aware of a sense of peace that could only come from him, and she realized that this was her answer.

"If God wore a polo shirt, then I felt like I was resting in his front pocket, dark but safe."[13] She still lives with the illness today, but God has given her a piece (peace) of himself that assures her of his presence. Even though some of the darkness is still there, she is safe in that pocket.

Trusting God's presence in the midst of his silence is a very important part of learning to trust his silence. So, before we leave this subject, let's look at a few more verses that reinforce this important principle. There are many to choose from, but here are some of my favorites:

> "God is our refuge and strength, an *ever-present* help in trouble" (Psalm 46:1, NIV, emphasis mine). The NASB version uses the phrase "a very present help", or "abundantly available".

> "GOD . . . never turns away from his friends." (Psalm 37:28, MSG)

> "He has never let you down, never looked the other way . . . never wandered off to do his own thing; he has been right there, listening" (Psalm 22:22-24, MSG). Notice that this passage comes toward the end of the chapter that began with "My God, my God, why have you abandoned me?"!

> " . . . the Master won't ever walk out and fail to return. If he works severely, he also works tenderly. His stockpiles of loyal love are immense. He takes no pleasure in making life hard, in throwing roadblocks in the way." (Lamentations 3:31-33, MSG)

Look up the following passages and write down every place or experience that is mentioned where we can count on God to be with us:

Psalm 139:7–10 _____

_____

_____

Romans 8:35–39 _____

_____

_____

What these verses reinforce is that there is sometimes a difference between reality and our perception of it. Our security needs to come from God's love rather than how we feel. No matter what it *feels* like, it is impossible to be separated from God. We are always in God's presence, and he is always present with us. Trusting his presence makes all the difference during the times when he chooses to be silent in our lives.

When we are faced with God's silence, we have a choice to make. We can embrace the silence or deny it and try to rush through it. Pete Greig says "how very fragile our faith must be if we can't just remain sad, scared, confused and doubting for a while. In our fear of unknowing, we leapfrog Holy Saturday and rush the resurrection. We race disconcerted to make meaning and find beauty where there simply is none. Yet."[14] In Feinberg's experience, she discovered that she had drawn a line with God, something that was simple and straightforward and made her feel safe. But, unfortunately, lines can become boundaries of self-protection—with God safely on one side and us on the other.[15] We erase the lines when we restore the truth about God in our hearts and focus on who he really is rather than who he appears to be in the silence. When God is silent, we can choose to remember former revelations of God in both the Bible and our own lives and trust the truth of those revelations even if they are a distant memory at the moment. This reminds me of a simple song we used to sing in worship:

"Never doubt in the darkness
What God has shown you in the light.
Fear may come to trouble you,
And you may not see too clearly
As it tries to take the little faith you know.
So never doubt in the darkness
What God has shown you in the light."[16]

I'm also reminded of John Bunyan's words in *The Pilgrim's Progress:* "These troubles and distresses that you go through in these waters are no sign that God hath forsaken you, but are sent to try you whether you will call to mind that which heretofore you have received of his goodness, and live upon him in your distresses."[17] Sometimes we just need to listen more carefully and wait more patiently while focusing on the truth that we know about God instead of the perception of him that the silence conveys.

Look up these verses and write what actions we are told to have before God:

Psalm 37:7a _____
Psalm 46:10 _____
Isaiah 30:15 _____
Micah 7:7 _____

Here are the words (from different translations) that stick out to me, maybe because most of them don't come naturally to me: be still, wait patiently, rest, quiet down, settle down, wait confidently, let go, relax, cease striving. To know God (see Psalm 46:10) is to acknowledge him for who he is; and we are to wait for God "in quietness and confidence" (see Isaiah 30:15, NLT), "counting on God to listen" to us (see Micah 7:7, MSG). This is the essence of faith, the real meaning of trusting God's silence.

When we choose to trust God's silence, our faithfulness expressed in perseverance becomes a powerful tool against the enemy. Instead of giving in to the lie that God has left us, we discover that, as C.S. Lewis said, Satan's cause "is never in more danger than when a human—no longer desiring but still intending to do [God's] will—looks round upon a universe from which every trace of Him seems to have vanished, and asks why he has been forsaken, and still obeys."[18] Then we are in a position for God to use our story of victory in future ministry for him in order to help others who are struggling with God's silence. According to Greig, "there is an anointing—an authority—that can only come to us through the darker trust of unanswered prayer . . . a healing that we can only minister when we have ourselves been wounded."[19] I want to be willing to persevere whenever God is silent in my life and continue to trust confidently in his presence and the value of his silence so that I can be victorious against the enemy and be used by God in the future in the lives of others. Will you choose to join me?

Describe an experience you have had with the silence of God. How did you feel? How did you respond? _____

_____

_____

_____

_____

What do you expect God's voice to sound like if he speaks to you? How do your expectations affect your response when he is silent? _

_____

_____

_____

_____

How does the reality of "God with us" make a difference in your faith when God is silent? _____

_____

_____

_____

_____

What might you need to focus on about God's character and previous work in your life in order to victoriously survive a time of God's silence in the future? _____

_____

_____

_____

_____

Lesson 12

Trusting God's Provision

We live in one of the most affluent cultures in history. As twenty-first century Americans, we have every imaginable luxury available to us; and these luxuries far exceed our level of need. If we don't have the immediate resources to obtain something, most of us are able to secure our needs and desires by paying for them over time. We truly can provide just about everything for ourselves without God's help. As a result, I think we sometimes miss allowing God to provide for us because we are too busy taking care of ourselves.

Some of the Old Testament characters and the early church in the New Testament didn't have the same options. Many of them understood better than we do what it means to depend on God to provide. Because of this, they did a better job of practicing community than we do, influenced as we are by our American Dream post-World War II society that glorifies independence. They knew how to use what God had given them to take care of everyone around them (see Acts 2:42-47 and 4:32-35).

I find it interesting that Christians are willing to trust God to provide for their souls but often find it difficult to entrust their physical needs to him. Somehow we have lost the necessary balance of understanding the need for each person to work to provide for himself (see 2 Thessalonians 3:6-10) and the recognition that all provision actually comes from God's hand. In our culture, it is easy to depend more on ourselves than we do on God; and this is where we get off track. So, before we go any further, let's look at some Bible passages that remind us who the source of everything really is:

"All the creatures look expectantly to you to give them their meals on time. You come, and they gather around; you open your hand and they eat from it. If you turned your back, they'd die in a minute—Take back your Spirit and they die, revert to original mud; Send out your Spirit and they spring to life—the whole countryside in bloom and blossom." (Psalm 104:27-30, MSG)

"Yours, O LORD, is the greatness and the power and the glory and the majesty and the splendor, for everything in heaven and earth is yours . . . Wealth and honor come from you; you are the ruler of all things. In your hands are strength and power to exalt and give strength to all . . . Everything comes from you, and we have given you only what comes from your hand . . . as for all this abundance that we have . . . it comes from your hand, and all of it belongs to you." (1 Chronicles 29:11-16, NIV)

"He himself gives life and breath to everything, and he satisfies every need." (Acts 17:25, NLT)

" . . . God, Who richly *and* ceaselessly provides us with everything for [our] enjoyment . . ." (1 Timothy 6:17, AMP)

"Every good and perfect gift is from above . . ." (James 1:17, NIV)

These verses help us to remember that everything comes from God and that all of creation is sustained by his care. Literally every breath we take is dependent on the life he has breathed into us, so our trust for provision should be in him alone rather than in ourselves. Since God is able to handle the needs of *all* of creation, he certainly is capable and sufficient to handle any needs we humans have. Even Jesus acknowledged that it is God who provides for us when he told us to pray, "Give us today our daily bread" (Matthew 6:11, NIV). Regardless of how hard we work or what we put into it, the Bible makes it clear that it is a misconception to think that we provide for ourselves. Constantly reminding ourselves of this truth is the first step to trusting God's provision in our lives.

The next thing we need to remember brings us once again to the difference between God's perspective and ours. Because we live in a physical world with tangible needs, we tend to forget that our physical and spiritual selves are intertwined. While we elevate our physical needs as the most important thing, God is equally interested in our spiritual needs. From his perspective, the two cannot be separated from each other.

Look up the following verses and write the words that show how God connects our physical and spiritual needs:

Psalm 37:4 _____

_____

Psalm 111:5 & 9 _____

_____

Isaiah 58:11 _____

_____

In Psalm 37:4, we see that the prerequisite for receiving the desires of our heart from God is to "delight" in him, which means to experience great pleasure and joy in his presence. We only experience great pleasure and joy in the presence of people that we know well, so this is a call to meaningful relationship with God. The NIV translation of the Psalm 111 passage also helps us connect the physical and spiritual: "He provides food for those who fear him . . . he provided redemption for his people". And, in Isaiah 58, we read that "the LORD will continually guide you, and satisfy your soul" (NASB).

This brings us to another part of God's perspective that might differ from ours: he will always provide for our *needs* but not necessarily our *wants*. Of course we all know this, but determining the difference between the two can sometimes be confusing from our earthly perspective. We can understand the difference between needs and wants better if we remember that our deepest needs are spiritual rather than physical. Everything God does in relation to humans revolves around helping us to recognize and embrace our utter dependence on him. Because our spiritual needs take precedence over our physical needs, God may sometimes allow us to go without some physical thing in order to grow more dependent on him spiritually. He wants us to learn that he is *enough* and that we need *him* more than we need anything else.

The well-known words of Psalm 23 illustrate this in the example of the complete dependence of sheep on their shepherd. Sheep can't do anything for themselves and must look to the shepherd to provide for all of their needs. David compares this to his relationship with God by saying, "The LORD is my shepherd; I have all that I need" (Ps. 23:1, NLT). David also acknowledges how God sometimes works in Psalm 34:10: "Even strong young lions sometimes go hungry, but those who trust in the LORD will lack no good thing" (NLT). *The Message* translation puts it this way: "GOD-seekers are full of God". We need to recognize the importance of being "full of God" instead of continually seeking to be full of earthly things.

The apostle Paul elaborated on this in his letter to the Philippian church: "I have strength for all things in Christ Who empowers me—I am ready for anything and equal to anything through Him Who infuses inner strength into me . . . my God will liberally supply (fill to the full) your every need . . ." (Phil. 4:13 & 19, AMP). Once again, we see that God will provide for our *needs*. What we want may be to feel good and avoid pain, but Paul shows us that God's provision may instead include the courage or strength we need to *face* the pain. Not only does God know best what our physical needs are, but he also knows best what our true spiritual needs are. Even when God's provision doesn't necessarily look good from our human standpoint, we need to trust his perspective and patiently wait for him to provide for us.

An exercise in God's perspective that we sometimes miss is to focus on what God has already provided for us instead of looking at what we still need him to provide. It is always helpful in our Christian walk to remind ourselves of God's goodness in the past and what the God of the universe, who owes nothing to any of us, has freely given to us. This type of focus on a daily basis can help us to trust him more fully for future provision, so let's look at some verses that help to jog our memories.

Remembering that both physical and spiritual needs are important to God, look up the following verses and list what he has already provided for every one of us:

Psalm 18:35 _____

_____

Psalm 40:2 _____

_____

Psalm 119:49 _____

_____

Jeremiah 33:9 _____

_____

John 1:12 _____

_____

John 14:16 _____

John 14:27 _____

Acts 14:16-17 _____

Romans 5:5 _____

Romans 6:23 _____

Romans 12:6-8; 1 Corinthians 12:4-11; 1 Peter 4:10-11 _____

_____

Romans 15:5-6 _____

1 Corinthians 7:7 _____

1 Corinthians 10:13 _____

1 Corinthians 15:57 _____

Ephesians 2:8-9 _____

Colossians 2:9-10 _____

James 1:5 _____

2 Peter 1:3-4 _____

1 John 5:20 _____

If we want to be reminded of God's goodness in providing for us, we don't need to look any further. In fact, as Acts 14:16-17 tells us, no one should ever question God's role in caring for us: " . . . he made a good creation, poured down rain and gave bumper crops. When your bellies were full and your hearts happy, there was *evidence of good beyond your doing*" (MSG, emphasis mine). And, since God has given the ultimate sacrifice of his own Son to provide for our spiritual needs, we shouldn't have to be concerned about his future provision for us (nor should we expect anything else from him). But several of these passages show us that God goes beyond that original provision, so that "we can't round up enough containers to hold everything God generously pours into our lives through the Holy Spirit!" (Rom. 5:5, MSG). Look at 1 Cor. 10:13: "But God is faithful [to His Word and to His compassionate nature], and He [can be trusted] not to let you be tempted *and* tried *and* assayed beyond your ability *and* strength of resistance *and* power to endure, but with the temptation He will [always] also provide the way out—the means of escape to a landing place—that you may be capable *and* strong *and* powerful patiently to bear up under it" (AMP). Now that's what I call provision! But God doesn't stop there. We see that "the Son of God came so we could recognize and understand the truth of God—what a gift!" (1 John 5:20, MSG) and that we are complete spiritually, having the full power and presence of God living in us (Col. 2:10) and possessing all of the resources we need to be truly godly (2 Peter 1:3-4). We need to never forget that God is not obligated to provide any of these things for us; but he does so out of his love for us and his desire to have a relationship with each one of his creations.

When we are reminded of this exhaustive list of things that God has already given us, it seems impossible that we could ever struggle with trusting him to provide for us in the future; but we do. Besides our own natural bent to self-centeredness, I think one of the reasons for this has to do with the way in which God chooses to provide for us. Sometimes God provides for us in miraculous ways, and sometimes he uses more common, everyday means. If we are always looking for miracles, we may miss the common ways he works; and if we are accustomed to thinking in earthly terms, we may miss a miracle God wants to perform. I have experienced numerous examples of

God's provision in both of these ways, so allow me to share several of them with you.

I don't believe in coincidences. Because God is sovereign over all creation, I believe that everything that happens could more appropriately be called a "God-incidence". Our family's experience with God has shown us that he cares deeply for us and can be trusted to provide for us at all times—but not always in the same way. The very specific nature of some of the incidences of God's provision for us has left no doubt in our minds that it was clearly God who was the provider regardless of how he may have used other people or circumstances in the process.

During times of unemployment or inadequate employment, we received numerous anonymous gifts of both food and money from members of our church body that always met the need we had at that exact moment. Examples of this include:

1) the time I used the last bit of flour we had to prepare our evening meal, knowing I had no way to buy more—only to have two of our deacons knock on our door a few minutes later to deliver bags of groceries which, to our delight, included five pounds of flour (the only time we ever received flour in a gift of food);

2) the donation by someone of the payment of our son's Christian school tuition when we didn't have enough money to cover it—which no one but us (and God!) specifically knew;

3) the gift on more than one occasion of a vehicle, either free or at a very low rate, which met our need at that precise point in time until we could buy something for ourselves.

Then there are the examples of God's exact provision in our lives that further defied logic and pointed us to him. (In reading these stories, you need to understand that I am not by nature a social being and that the *specific* needs we had at these times were known only to God and our family. We had neither shared our need nor solicited help from anyone except God.)

During my twelve-week treatment for cancer, I had one week of break between sets of radiation. Ron and I strongly felt the need to get away for a couple of days for a respite, but we didn't really have the extra money to do so. We made a reservation for a two-night stay at a nearby island resort, using a 2-for-1 coupon that we had received. The trip would cost us about $100. The day before we left, I discovered a crisp $100 bill that had been tucked in my Bible on the previous Sunday by someone at church who listened to God's leading without fully understanding everything God was doing.

Another time, Ron's cousin was dying in a hospital about eighty miles away, and Ron planned to visit him after church (by himself) on Sunday afternoon; but, on Saturday morning, Ron felt compelled to not wait until the following day. However, Saturdays were family days; and for our young family to be separated didn't seem like the right thing to do. So, even though we didn't know how we would replace the money by the time we needed it, the four of us rode the ferry to Seattle and made a frugal but fun family day out of a serious situation. God confirmed the Spirit's leading when Ron's cousin passed away during the night on Saturday and he was the last person to talk to him about his relationship with God. But he further confirmed our commitment to family and our trust in him when I played the piano for a memorial service at our church the following week (a common practice for me) and received twice as much monetary provision as usual—the exact amount that we had spent the previous weekend. I experienced a similar example of God's provision on another occasion when a good friend's daughter was having heart surgery and I chose to travel to the hospital to pray with them and support them.

Once, when I was balancing our checkbook against our monthly statement, I discovered that the amounts were exactly $100 off from each other—in our favor. Upon research, I found that a $100 hold that had previously been required on all accounts had been discontinued, and the money that I had placed in my account at the age of fifteen was now ours to use as we liked. Not surprisingly, we were $100 short of providing for our needs during the month that this occurred, and God had once again shown his sovereignty over every area of our lives.

Maybe you've never experienced this type of miraculous provision from God. God doesn't work the same way all of the time; and our family's experiences with miracles may be difficult for you to understand. During our needy years when my husband was the sole wage-earner in our family, I could have worked outside the home and supplemented his income with more than a one-evening-a-week piano teaching career. But behind the need for God to provide miraculously for us was our unwavering commitment and belief that God's design for our family while our children were being raised was for me to be a fulltime homemaker. We determined from the moment our first son was born that we would not get in God's way and take human measures to provide for ourselves if they stepped outside of our commitment for my career as a homemaker. Because of this, trust played a key role in our whole approach to life. So these examples of God's provision for us not only gave us what we needed physically, but they also confirmed this belief and commitment we had made.

The Bible gives us many examples of the role of trust when it comes to God's provision. In Malachi 3:8-12, God challenges the nation of Israel (and us!) to trust him enough to tithe regularly. Apparently it was as easy for them as it can be for us to hang onto what God has given and fail to trust him to provide with more instead of freely giving tithes and offerings and trusting him to take care of his people. Regardless of what our lives look like on paper, the Biblical principle remains the same: God owns everything and our tithes and offerings are only returning to him a portion of what is already his. The degree to which trust enters into this process will differ for everyone, but there is always something else that we could spend our money on besides choosing to return some of it to God.

The classic Biblical story of God's provision occurs in Genesis 22:1-14, when Abraham was asked by God to physically sacrifice his much-loved son Isaac on an altar. Read this passage of Scripture and then answer the following questions:

According to verse 1, why did God ask Abraham to sacrifice Isaac?

_____

_____

What do Abraham's actions in verses 3 and 10 tell us about his heart?

_____

_____

What does Abraham's response to Isaac in verse 8 tell us about his faith? _____

_____

_____

In our culture, it is difficult to understand this story; but the lessons from it are just as important for our day as for Abraham. God wants our trust in him to be complete and solid rather than wavering in response to life's circumstances. Abraham's faith was confirmed and his heart-commitment to obey God deepened through this event, which had nothing to do with actually sacrificing his son. Since God had told Abraham that Isaac was the means to countless descendents, he must have wondered what God was doing by asking him to kill Isaac; and, since Mt. Moriah was fifty to sixty miles from where he lived, Abraham had plenty of time to think about everything and turn back. His firm belief that "God will provide" is a timeless example for all generations after him of the importance of trusting God for absolutely everything.

Sometimes God's provision for us does not occur in miraculous ways. In fact, sometimes God's method of providing doesn't feel positive to us; but we can still trust his hand in our lives. In the Old Testament, Joseph's brothers hated him so much that they sold him into slavery in Egypt, thinking they would never see him again. Many years later, they were reunited when Joseph's brothers traveled to Egypt to find food during a severe famine and discovered that Joseph was in charge of the food distribution for the whole country. Joseph tells his brothers, "You intended to harm me, but God intended it all for good. He brought me to this position so I could save the lives of many people" (Genesis 50:20, NLT). And, while the brothers' trip to Egypt eventually resulted in the Israelites' slavery in Egypt for four hundred years, God provided for his people and preserved the nation of Israel through it all. Some of the ways God has provided for our family are similar.

> During the same timeframe of many of God's miraculous provisions in our lives, my husband took on a second job in a janitorial position for a large public utility. This was night work every day of the week that proved quickly to be too exhaustive for him to continue while working fulltime elsewhere during the day. However, during his short tenure there, he received the recommendation of a worker at the utility to a local orthodontist who was

looking for weekly janitorial service at his office. For over ten years, our family went together one evening a week to the orthodontist's office and cleaned, each person with his/her own age-appropriate jobs. And God provided not only for our immediate financial needs but also the ability to teach our children (outside of chores at home) a proper work ethic. Beyond that, we discovered soon after we began this journey that both of our children required extensive orthodontic work (for physically functional rather than purely aesthetic reasons) and that ALL of that work would be free of charge because we were employees of this doctor! While we didn't *enjoy* spending one night a week cleaning an office, we never wondered whether God was providing for us.

When our first son attended college, besides receiving scholarships and grants, he took out several private student loans on top of his federal ones to help pay for his education, with us as his co-signers. This is pretty typical in our current culture; but, when our second son left home for college, things in our lives had changed drastically. Because of our bankruptcy, we were no longer able to get a loan for anything—including co-signing a student loan. The timing of our business failure meant that, for all of his undergraduate years, we were claiming a loss from our business on our income tax and paying no federal taxes. As a result, besides the scholarships he earned, he received numerous grants and federal loans that nearly completely covered his education at a private Christian college. The first year we paid taxes after our business closed was his senior year of college, which didn't affect his financial aid. God provided for us in an abnormal way—on the heels of great loss—but he still provided for us mightily.

Now that our children are grown and gone, God's provision for us has included employment for me outside the home. My heart is still at home, and I still long to be there fulltime. But God has provided a secure job for me with good benefits in an environment that is largely positive, and I choose most of the time to be grateful for that and to trust him to continue to provide for my spiritual and emotional needs as well.

What about God's provision for our future? In his instruction known as *The Lord's Prayer*, Jesus seems to point us away from planning for the future: "Give us today the food we need", or "our food for today" (Matthew 6:11, NLT); and the story in Exodus 16 where God provided manna for the Israelites is similar. The people had to do the work of gathering the manna; and, if they gathered more than what they needed for one day, the food spoiled. Yet we live in a society that expects us to have savings plans for college, for retirement, and for our heirs. How do we reconcile the two and follow what God wants us to do?

I don't have a definitive answer because I don't think it's the same for everyone. God provides for all of our needs, but he blesses some people with more provision than others. What we do with what he has provided should be an individual response of obedience based on our personal relationship with him. The important thing for all of us is to grow in our dependence on God, whatever that looks like individually. While our family has never been in a position to save much for the future (based on our strong commitment to a single wage-earner), God has still provided for every need and beyond in ways too numerous to count. We are very grateful for the opportunities we had to teach our children about God's provision through firsthand experiences over the years, and we believe he will continue to provide for us in the unknown future ahead. I think what God wants from all of us is the willingness to do whatever he has called us to do and to make sure we're not getting in his way as he provides for us. As Abraham showed us, obedience and trust go hand in hand.

Trusting God's provision and obeying his calling on our lives should produce obvious and tangible results. In Matthew 10:8, Jesus gives us a principle to live by: "Freely you have received, freely give" (NIV). *The Message* translation goes even further: "You have been treated generously, so live generously." If we trust God fully to provide for us, we have the freedom to be generous with what we have been given. God's generosity with us should lead to our generosity with others (see Philemon 6). When we trust God to provide for us, we don't have to worry about running out of resources. Look at these well-known words of Jesus from the Sermon on the Mount:

> "If you decide for God, living a life of God-worship, it follows that you don't fuss about what's on the table at mealtimes or whether the clothes in your closet are in fashion. There is far more to your life than the food you put in your stomach, more to your outer appearance than the clothes you hang on your body. Look at the birds, free and unfettered, not tied down to a job description, careless in the care of God. And you count far more to him than birds.

> Has anyone by fussing in front of the mirror ever gotten taller by so much as an inch? All this time and money wasted on fashion—do you think it makes that much difference? Instead of looking at the fashions, walk out into the fields and look at the wildflowers. They never primp or shop, but have you ever seen color and design quite like it? The ten best-dressed men and women in the country look shabby alongside them.

> If God gives such attention to the appearance of wildflowers—most of which are never even seen—don't

145

you think he'll attend to you, take pride in you, do his best for you? What I'm trying to do here is to get you to relax, to not be so preoccupied with *getting*, so you can respond to God's *giving*. People who don't know God and the way he works fuss over these things, but you know both God and how he works. Steep your life in God-reality, God-initiative, God-provisions. Don't worry about missing out. You'll find all your everyday human concerns will be met.

Give your entire attention to what God is doing right now, and don't get worked up about what may or may not happen tomorrow." (Matthew 6:25-34, MSG)

The language used in this translation is so descriptive. Jesus wants us to get rid of being preoccupied with earthly things, with fussing or getting worked up. Instead, he wants us to relax and live free, unfettered lives where we can be truly "careless" (without cares) and focus our attention in the right direction—toward God. Worry can damage health, disrupt productivity, negatively affect treatment of others, and reduce ability to trust God more. It is a vicious circle: not trusting God to provide actually produces less trust in the future. Worriers are consumed by fear and immobilized for action. God wants us to trust him for our provision for living so that we can focus our attention on more important things. Then we will be fully using all that he has given us in order to further his kingdom.

More than once the Bible gives us the picture of farming as an example of what our lives should look like. God doesn't want us to hide, devour, or throw away what he has given us. Instead, we are to cultivate his gifts like seeds: "And God will generously provide all you need. Then you will always have everything you need and plenty left over to share with others . . . for God is the one who provides seed for the farmer and then bread to eat. In the same way, he will provide and increase your resources and then produce a great harvest of generosity in you" (2 Corinthians 9:8 & 10, NLT). This includes physical as well as spiritual resources. God wants us to share generously with others whatever he has given us, whether money and other earthly possessions or spiritual gifts: "God doesn't want us to be shy with his gifts, but bold and loving and sensible" (2 Timothy 1:7, MSG). Truly trusting God's provision for us gives us the freedom to live as he intended us to live and to grow even more in faith as we watch him work in our lives and in the lives of those around us. Are you ready to step out in faith?

From the verses you looked up earlier in this lesson, what things that God has already provided for you are the most meaningful to you?

_____

_____

_____

How does focusing on these things help you to trust his future provision for you? _____

_____

_____

_____

How does Abraham's story in Genesis 22:1-14 encourage you to trust God's provision in *your* life? _____

_____

_____

_____

Are you more prone to worry about financial issues or to trust God to provide? How can you grow in your ability to trust God's provision so you can live a more carefree life? _____

_____

_____

_____

What is one step you can take to be more generous with what God has given you, either physical or spiritual resources? _____

_____

_____

_____

Lesson 13

Trusting God's Blessings

If you have been a Christian for very long at all, you recognize that you have received blessings from God that you didn't have before you chose to follow him. But, if you live in the real world, you also recognize that being a follower of God doesn't guarantee that every part of your life will always feel blessed. To begin to trust God's blessings requires that we define what a blessing is and determine what the Bible says we can expect, which also includes figuring out what we should *not* expect. This is where we discover that the world's definition and God's definition of blessing are not the same.

The dictionary defines blessing as prosperity, success, or anything that brings comfort and happiness or prevents misfortune. When we align our thinking with this definition, we expect laughter, pleasure, or earthly prosperity, including an immunity to failure or difficulties and a guarantee of health, wealth, and happiness. This type of thinking can sometimes lead to greed, pride, and a false sense of security. When the events of our lives don't match up with our definition of blessing, we can begin to doubt God's presence or whether he's paying attention to us at all; and doubt is one of Satan's greatest strongholds in our lives.

The Bible shows us that God defines blessing differently. For the Christian, blessings refer to God's gifts to us, which include security, freedom from fear, strength, peace, and the experience of hope and joy independent of our outward circumstances. We can expect God's blessing to include guidance (see Psalm 1:1-3) and discipline (see Psalm 94:12) as well as comfort, mercy, and the keys to the Kingdom of Heaven (see Matthew 5:3-12 and Luke 12:32). To be blessed by God means to have a distinctive spiritual joy and ultimate well-being that only comes from relationship with him. It is the state of being *spiritually* prosperous, an inner condition that should affect our outward behavior and approach to life. As Christians, the blessings and benefits we seek should be different than those that other people want to achieve. The Bible verses known as *The Beatitudes* (literally, "declarations of blessedness"), which are a portion of Christ's Sermon on the Mount, reinforce this contrast between the world's values and God's values, the difference between what is temporary and what is eternal:

> "You're blessed when you're at the end of your rope. With less of you there is more of God and his rule.
>
> You're blessed when you feel you've lost what is most dear to you. Only then can you be embraced by the One most dear to you.
>
> You're blessed when you're content with just who you are— no more, no less. That's the moment you find yourselves proud owners of everything that can't be bought.
>
> You're blessed when you've worked up a good appetite for God. He's food and drink in the best meal you'll ever eat.
>
> You're blessed when you care. At the moment of being 'care-full', you find yourselves cared for.

You're blessed when you get your inside world—your mind and heart—put right. Then you can see God in the outside world.

You're blessed when you can show people how to cooperate instead of compete or fight. That's when you discover who you really are, and your place in God's family.

You're blessed when your commitment to God provokes persecution. The persecution drives you even deeper into God's kingdom.

Not only that—count yourselves blessed every time people put you down or throw you out or speak lies about you to discredit me. What it means is that the truth is too close for comfort and they are uncomfortable. You can be glad when that happens—give a cheer, even!—for though they don't like it, *I* do! And all heaven applauds." Matthew 5:3-12, MSG)

If there are two different definitions of what blessing is and therefore two different expectations of what life will consist of, it follows that our behavior and approach to life will be affected by our definition. Assuming that we want *God's* blessings more than *earthly* blessings, we find in the Bible that there are conditions for us and choices we need to make.

Look up the following verses and write what type of person can expect God's blessings:

Psalm 1:1-3 _____

_____

Psalm 5:12 _____

_____

Psalm 84:11-12 _____

_____

Psalm 112:1-9 _____

_____

Psalm 115:12-13 _____

_____

Psalm 119:1-2 _____

_____

Psalm 128:1-4 _____

_____

Psalm 133 _____

_____

Proverbs 3:13 _____

_____

Proverbs 3:33 _____

_____

Proverbs 10:6a _____

_____

Proverbs 28:20 _____

_____

Jeremiah 17:7-8 _____

_____

James 1:12 _____

_____

James 1:25 _____

_____

Did you notice a theme here? It's pretty clear that God's blessings are reserved for those who are serious about a relationship with him. While God's sovereignty is involved in his decisions to bestow blessings (see Exodus 33:19), and while we can definitely trust his heart's desire to be generous and freely give to us (see previous Lesson 4—*Trusting God's Thoughts Toward You*), these verses leave no doubt that the condition of *our* hearts matters to him when he chooses who to bless. Faithful obedience, a heart that diligently tries to obey God's will, and response to God's revealed and written Word are all characteristics of the one who is blessed by God. The different words used in the *New International Version* translation of Psalm 1:1-3 help us to understand what this means. To "stand" means to *station* yourself, while to "sit" means to *settle* yourself; and "walk in" means to *order your life according to*. God doesn't expect perfect sin-free living, but he does want us to position ourselves in such a way that we are seeking him and always trying to follow his Word.

As *The Beatitudes* show us, what matters to God is heartfelt obedience rather than legalistic observance to a set of rules. The meek and poor in spirit are humble before God instead of spiritually proud or self-sufficient. The people who get in on God's blessings are those whose interests and loyalties are not divided, who have a deep passion for personal righteousness and a dissatisfaction with present spiritual attainment, and who anguish over sin and desire to be peaceful, like God.[1] They are fully-devoted followers of God.

When Abraham was willing to follow God even to the point of sacrificing his own son (discussed more fully in Lesson 12— *Trusting God's Provision*), God gave him many blessings because of his obedience (see Genesis 22:15-18). Likewise, the Israelites were promised an amazing list of blessings if they would choose to fully obey God (which they did not).

Read Deuteronomy 28:1-14 and list all of the blessings that God promised to the Israelites. _____

_____

_____

_____

_____

_____

I am struck by how apparent God's heart is in this long list of blessings. He clearly wanted to give generously to the Israelites, and we can still trust his unchanging heart today in the world we live in.

To help you understand and trust God's heart better, look again at these verses from above and list each blessing that God will give:

Psalm 1:3 _____

_____

Psalm 5:12 _____

_____

Psalm 128:2-3 _____

_____

Jeremiah 17:8 _____

_____

Matthew 5:3-10 _____

_____

_____

James 1:12 _____

_____

The list you have created just scratches the surface of what blessings are available to those who choose to obey God and trust him; but it is a good reminder of what God is like and how he longs to give good things to us. Hopefully this list encourages you to walk closely with him each step of the way.

Earlier, I mentioned the role of God's sovereignty in his choice to bless us; but let's talk more about why God blesses and why he sometimes holds back blessings. Remember, God always has a purpose behind what he does even if we can't see it clearly or understand it completely (see Lesson 6—*Trusting God's Purposes*). First of all, while we tend to think of blessings as things that we get to enjoy *right now*, God's blessings often involve future generations and may even stretch into eternity.

Look up the following verses and list who is included in the blessing that God is giving:

Genesis 22:15-18 _____

_____

Psalm 67:1-2 & 7 _____

_____

Galatians 3:9 _____

_____

As you can see, God's blessings are not isolated to the specific individuals he blesses at any given time. When God blessed Abraham for his obedience in Genesis 22, the blessing included all of the Israelite people and also all future people who would choose to obey God. It was an extension of God's original blessing on all of mankind before sin entered the world in the garden (see Genesis 1:28) that had been renewed with Abraham when God called him in Genesis 12:1-3. We are included in this and are blessed now and into eternity because of God's blessing on Abraham nearly five thousand years ago! God's blessing on his people is what sets them apart and helps to show the rest of the world a little of his grace and glory.

The story of Job also helps us to recognize the need to trust God's purposes in his decisions to bless or withhold blessing. God does not allow us to suffer for no reason, but he is also not limited by our expectations of what a blessing is. At the end of Job's difficult ordeal of loss and suffering, God blessed Job again because the reason for his suffering was complete. In Job 42:12-17, we see that God blessed Job much more in the second part of his life than he had in the first; and he lived to be a very old man. The previous losses, though real and painful, were not the end of the story. We have to remember this: just because God's purposes may be hidden from us doesn't mean they don't exist. And we also have to remember that God's ability to bless in an eternal way far exceeds our limited expectations for him to bless us in the here and now.

Which leads us to one of the main reasons that God chooses to withhold blessing sometimes from our lives: " . . . He may deprive us of *something* in order to draw us to *Someone*."[2] While God loves to bless us, he is much more interested in relationships than blessings. Often he may hold back blessing in our lives for a time so that we will draw nearer to him and learn something new about his character or his way of doing things. God is always interested in our spiritual growth above anything else, and he wants our relationship with him to grow as he continually prepares us for eternity with him. From his eternal perspective, nothing is more important.

As we have seen repeatedly in previous chapters, the difference between God's perspective and ours often gets in the way of our growth. When it comes to God's blessings, we sometimes need to take a step back and recognize the constant blessing God gives by continuing to be present in our world and by keeping his hand and control on everything. We simply have no concept of what it would mean and how our lives would be different if God removed his hand; and we cannot fully understand what it means to be blessed by God. Our view is extremely limited.

Previously, we looked at Psalms 84:11-12 and 112:1-9. Both of these passages focus on what is important from God's perspective: regardless of the presence of darkness and bad news, the one who trusts God has a *heart* that is steadfast and secure (Ps. 112). In the language that is used in Psalm 84, we see that God blesses us with everything that is *permanently* good, not necessarily with everything that *we* think is good; and he won't hold back anything from us that will help us to serve him better. We live in a fallen world, so our experience—even with God's blessings—will be imperfect from our perspective. But, thankfully,

> "We are pressed on every side by troubles, but we are not crushed . . . we suffer embarrassments *and* are perplexed *and* unable to find a way out, but not driven to despair . . . We are hunted down, but never abandoned by God. We get knocked down, but we are not destroyed . . . Even though on the outside it often looks like things are falling apart on us . . . the inside, where God is making new life, is being (progressively) renewed day after day . . . There's far more here than meets the eye. The things we see now are here today, gone tomorrow. But the things we can't

see now will last forever." (2 Corinthians 4:8-9, 16, 18, NLT, AMP, and MSG)

Looking at things from God's eternal perspective means that our response to God's way of blessing us must include trusting closed doors as well as opened ones and choosing to believe that God is blessing regardless of what it looks like to us. While we tend to have an "if this, then this" mentality, we have to remember that God doesn't work that way. Following God does not guarantee that everything that we can see will always seem like a blessing or that our efforts will be blessed by God in the way that we envision. God's blessings come from his character, so his traits of omnipresence (present everywhere), omniscience (all-knowing), and omnipotence (all-powerful) are at work when he blesses us. Those aspects are what connect his eternal perspective with our present perspective; and trusting those character traits is what helps us to trust God's blessings in our lives even when those blessings seem to be hidden within bad things from our perspective.

When our business failed, I struggled for a long time because my concept of God's blessing was incorrect. We believed that our business was God's will, so I naively expected that God would continue to bless its operation despite changes in the local economy or our mistakes as owners. I had decided what God's blessing would look like, which for me meant a financially successful business. But, over the past five years since the business closed, I have come to recognize in a new way the importance of letting God work in his own way; and my relationship with him has grown as a result. My faith has been transformed in ways that would not have occurred if our business was still open and financially secure, and this is more important to God than any amount of monetary or physical blessings.

God's eternal perspective on blessings was further illustrated to us in the financial ramifications that we faced following the business closure. Filing bankruptcy is a difficult decision and not viewed favorably by people in our society. But, because of the way that bankruptcy law is written, our bankruptcy to alleviate the debt from our business also brought us relief from some personal debts. While the method seemed negative and continues to affect us today, God blessed us with the freedom to live debt-free for the first time in years. Every day, we can choose to focus on the negative aspects of bankruptcy or recognize God's hand in blessing us through the process. When we were forced to sell our home to avoid foreclosure, God blessed us by bringing an acquaintance to buy it (at the eleventh hour) who gave us a fair price and kept us from adding the stigma of foreclosure to our financial resume. While we still had to deal with the emotional effects of losing our house, God's blessing included sparing us at least *some* of the long-term effects that could have been part of that event.

We can always choose how to respond to what happens to us and decide whether to focus on what is negative or on God's blessings. We can also choose on a daily basis to have a "gratitude attitude"[3] in our journey through life, focusing on how God has already blessed us instead of being greedy for more of his blessings. " . . . (T)here will always be blessings for which we can be grateful and in which we can discern the faithfulness and goodness of God."[4] This involves employing our memories and may include actively choosing to remember and be thankful for all of God's past blessings in our lives, beginning with Christ's original sacrifice for our sin and continuing to include the full range of everyday blessings that each of us has been given. As we see in John 1:16, we shouldn't have to look very far to have a long list of blessings to be thankful for: "For out of His fullness (abundance) we all received—all had a share and we were all supplied with—one grace after another *and* spiritual blessing upon spiritual blessing, *and* even favor upon favor *and* gift [heaped] upon gift" (AMP). We all have the complete package of benefits connected with knowing God: we have been chosen, adopted, and forgiven, and have spiritual insight, spiritual gifts, the power to do God's will, and a future hope. And we get to enjoy these blessings now and not just in the future because we have a personal relationship with the God of the universe, the supplier of all of these blessings. "All praise to God, the Father of our Lord Jesus Christ, who has blessed us with every spiritual blessing in the heavenly realms because we are united with Christ" (Ephesians 1:3, NLT).

Regardless of your perception of the presence or lack of *earthly* blessings in your life, focusing your attention in the right direction should produce a grateful heart and a different perspective on how your life is truly blessed in all the ways that *really* matter. Yes, we all have to live in the here and now; and sometimes God's blessings are hard to see. But God is always calling us, through all of life's ups and downs, to the higher goal of living in his presence and looking at things through *his* eyes. He wants us to trust his heart and reach a place where "we live by faith, not by sight" (2 Corinthians 5:7, NIV).

Honestly describe your definition on being "blessed" when you began this lesson. What characteristics did you expect a blessed life to include? _____

_____

_____

_____

Reread *The Message* translation of Matthew 5:3–12 at the beginning of this lesson. Which of *The Beatitudes* speaks most directly to your life circumstances, either past or present? What do you find here that most encourages you? _____

_____

_____

_____

What experience in your life has led you to doubt God's blessing in the past? How could focusing on God's perspective have changed your response? _____

_____

_____

_____

Take some time and make a list of every blessing you have received from God throughout your life, including those that all Christians enjoy as well as those specific to your own situation. After you have finished your list, spend some time thanking God for his goodness and expressing your love to him.

Afterword

It has been nearly eighteen months since I began the active process of writing this book, and the journey is now almost completed. I have loved every minute of it! The studying of God's Word was exhilarating, and the process of putting everything together into organized structure was exciting. I felt God's presence and guidance every step of the way. Yes, it was hard work; but I am grateful I didn't have to rely on my own power alone to accomplish the task. Instead, I could trust God's Spirit to illuminate his Word for me and his strength to keep me persevering to the end.

My husband Ron's patience during this project cannot be overstated. Since I work outside the home, my writing primarily occurred on the weekends—nearly every weekend for over a year. I am very grateful for Ron's willingness to support God's call on my life and accept many hours alone on Saturdays in order for me to finish what God started.

I began this study with the statement that everything in life is about faith and trust. I believe that more today than when I first wrote it. As I neared the end of this project, I faced numerous attacks from the enemy and the expectation from God that I would exercise even more faith. During this time, both of my children faced major life changes; and, not surprisingly, I discovered that the publishing part of writing a book about faith also requires a good amount of faith!

Faith is a lifelong journey, and everyone is on a slightly different path. That's why faith is not always simple and not always a foregone conclusion, and every honest Christ-follower has to come to terms with this side of faith sometime or maybe at many times during the journey. While the ultimate goal for all of us is complete Christlikeness, the process to get there not only involves the transformation of our minds but also what Philippians 2:12-13 speaks about—working *out* our salvation as God works *in* us:

> "Work hard to show the results of your salvation, obeying God with deep reverence and fear. For God is working in you, giving you the desire and the power to do what pleases him." (NLT)

The Amplified New Testament translation reminds us that working out our salvation means to "cultivate, carry out to the goal and fully complete", in partnership with God, who is "all the while effectually at work in you—energizing and creating in you the power and desire . . .". Faith and obedience cannot be separated, but working out our faith on a daily basis may sometimes involve questioning and struggling along the way. We should not be surprised or afraid when our faith is tested and we are asked by God to exercise even more faith. As Hebrews 11:1 points out, "Faith is the confidence that what we hope for will actually happen; it gives us assurance about things we cannot see" (NLT).

Prior to this verse, the writer of Hebrews reminds us that our faith is grounded in a secure and immovable anchor of hope, "an unbreakable spiritual lifeline" (Hebrews 6:19, MSG). The beginning point of faith is trust in God's character, and the endpoint is trusting his promises (see Hebrews 10:23). God *is* who he says he is, so we know that he will *do* what he says he will. True faith means trusting in God without actually seeing the end result, so living by faith and not by sight may involve struggles and hard work.

I have talked a lot in this study about the difference between God's perspective and our perspective. While this may seem redundant to some, I don't think this point can be over-emphasized. The things that matter to God are so different and so much deeper than what often matters to us, and this affects our walk of faith. To be honest, while I always trust the destination where God is taking me, I sometimes fear the journey to get there. I know the outcome will be the best from *God's* perspective, but I also know that the process may involve pain from *my* perspective. This is when I have to choose to look beyond the present to focus on God's ultimate work in me, " . . . being confident of this, that he who began a good work in you will carry it on to completion . . ." (Philippians 1:6, NIV).

Everything in life is about faith, and faith is ultimately all about focus. At the end of an exhaustive list of past people of faith in Hebrews 11, the writer helps us to remember that the Christian life is a long-distance race rather than a short sprint and that we need to be encouraged by the lives of those who have struggled with faith prior to us in order to keep faithfully running. Since Christ is both the start and the finish of our faith-race, weariness and discouragement can be overcome by properly fixing our eyes on him. Just as a runner who looks at his feet, we will surely stumble if we look at ourselves or our circumstances.

> "Therefore, since we are surrounded by such a huge crowd of witnesses to the life of faith, let us throw off everything that hinders and the sin that so easily entangles, and let us run with patient endurance *and* steady *and* active persistence the race God has set before us. We do this by keeping our eyes on Jesus, Who is the Leader *and* the Source of *our* faith [giving the first incentive for our belief] and is also its Finisher, [bringing it to maturity and perfection] . . . Think of all the hostility he endured from sinful people; then you won't become weary and give up." (Hebrews 12:1-3, NLT, NIV, AMP)

As this part of *my* faith journey is completed, I trust that my eyes have been fixed on Jesus and hope that you have been encouraged to do the same. I am extremely grateful to God for his work in me and humbled that he would choose to use me in spite of all my flaws. My prayer for this book continues to be that he would receive the glory that he deserves as he works in you and continues to complete the work he has begun in you.

Notes

Throughout the book, the author is indebted to the following two resources for some of the thoughts presented herein:

Kenneth Barker, ed., *The NIV Study Bible: New International Version* (Grand Rapids: Zondervan Bible Publishers, 1985).

Life Application Study Bible: New Living Translation (Wheaton: Tyndale House Publishers, 2004).

Lesson 1 ~ *What's Faith Got to Do With It?*
1. Amy Grant and Wes King, *We Believe in God* (Age to Age Music and Locally Owned Music, 1992).

Lesson 2 ~ *Trusting God's Word*
1. Merrill F. Unger, *Unger's Bible Dictionary* (Chicago: Moody Press, 1966), 340-341.
2. See Beth Moore, *Praying God's Word: Breaking Free from Spiritual Strongholds* (Nashville: Broadman & Holman Publishers, 2000).

Lesson 3 ~ *Trusting God's Sovereignty*
1. Unger, *Unger's Bible Dictionary,* 1041.
2. Eugene H. Peterson, *THE MESSAGE: The Bible in Contemporary Language* (Colorado Springs: NavPress, 2002), 19.
3. Ibid, 457.
4. Shannon J. Wexelberg, *I Am Undone* (Shanny Banny Music/ McKinney Music, 2009).

5. See E. Michael and Sharon Rusten, *The One Year Book of Christian History: A Daily Glimpse Into God's Powerful Work* (Wheaton: Tyndale House Publishers, 2003).
6. Peterson, *THE MESSAGE,* 560 and 1743.

Lesson 4 ~ *Trusting God's Thoughts Toward You*
1. *Life Application Study Bible,* 1953.
2. Barker, ed., *The NIV Study Bible,* 932.
3. Peterson, *THE MESSAGE,* 1608.
4. See Charles R. Swindoll, *You and Your Child* (Nashville: Thomas Nelson Publishers, 1977).
5. James I. Packer, Merrill C. Tenney, and William White, Jr., eds., *The Bible Almanac* (Nashville: Thomas Nelson Publishers, 1980), 413.
6. Peterson, *THE MESSAGE,* 449.
7. Ibid, 457.
8. Ibid, 405.

Lesson 5 ~ *Trusting God's Grace*
1. Eugene H. Peterson, *Practice Resurrection: A Conversation on Growing Up In Christ* (Grand Rapids: William B. Eerdmans Publishing Company, 2010), 94.
2. Ibid, 63.
3. See Michael Card, *A Violent Grace* (Sisters: Multnomah Publishers, 2000).
4. See Carol Hamblet Adams, *My Beautiful Broken Shell: Words of Hope to Refresh the Soul* (Eugene: Harvest House Publishers, 1998).
5. Peterson, *Practice Resurrection,* 95.
6. Ibid, 96.
7. Ibid, 98-106.

Lesson 6 ~ *Trusting God's Purposes*
1. Peterson, *THE MESSAGE,* 561.
2. See Henry T. Blackaby and Claude V. King, *Experiencing God: Knowing & Doing the Will of God* (Nashville: LifeWay Press, 1990).

3. Peterson, *THE MESSAGE*, 458.
4. Ibid, 1201.
5. Ibid, 837.
6. See Chuck Girard, *All I Want* (Dunamis Music, 1977).
7. Peterson, *THE MESSAGE*, 362.
8. Ibid, 1162, emphasis mine.
9. Ibid, 561 and 1684.

Lesson 7 ~ *Trusting God's Timing*
1. Taken from the booklet by the same name by Charles E. Hummel (originally published in 1967, republished by InterVarsity Press, 1999).
2. Margaret Feinberg, *The Sacred Echo: Hearing God's Voice in Every Area of Your Life* (Grand Rapids: Zondervan, 2008), 61.
3. Ibid, 59.
4. Ibid, 63.
5. Ibid, 65.
6. Ibid, 66.
7. Ibid, 65.
8. Ibid, 69.
9. See Beth Moore, *Get Out of That Pit: Straight Talk about God's Deliverance* (Nashville: Integrity Publishers, 2007).

Lesson 8 ~ *Trusting God's Protection*
1. J.I. Packer, *A Quest for Godliness: The Puritan Vision of the Christian Life* (Wheaton: Crossway, 1990), 33.
2. Unger, *Unger's Bible Dictionary*, 208.
3. Beth Moore, *Stepping Up: A Journey Through the Psalms of Ascent* (Nashville: LifeWay Press, 2007), 29.
4. See C.S. Lewis, *The Screwtape Letters, Revised Edition* (New York: Collier Books, MacMillan Publishing Company, 1982).
5. See Max Lucado, *Cosmic Christmas* (Nashville: Word Publishing, 1997).

6. Roy Lessin (taken from a framed picture produced by DaySpring).
7. Moore, *Stepping Up*, 24.

Lesson 9 ~ *Trusting God Through Loss*
1. Eugene H. Peterson, *A Long Obedience in the Same Direction: Discipleship in an Instant Society* (Downers Grove: InterVarsity Press, 2000), 136.
2. Ibid, 144-145.
3. Moore, *Stepping Up*, 128.
4. Peterson, *A Long Obedience in the Same Direction,* 141 and 145.
5. Moore, *Stepping Up*, 129.

Lesson 10 ~ *Trusting God Through Changes*
1. Peterson, *THE MESSAGE,* 838.
2. Miriam Webster, *Made Me Glad* (Hillsong Australia).

Lesson 11 ~ *Trusting God's Silence*
1. Eugene H. Peterson, *Christ Plays in Ten Thousand Places: A Conversation in Spiritual Theology* (Grand Rapids: William B. Eerdmans Publishing Company, 2005), 154.
2. Feinberg, *The Sacred Echo,* 169.
3. Peterson, *Christ Plays in Ten Thousand Places,* 156.
4. Ibid, 153.
5. Pete Greig, *God on Mute: Engaging the Silence of Unanswered Prayer* (Ventura: Regal Books, 2007), 202.
6. Ibid, 194.
7. Ibid, 197.
8. Ibid, 198.
9. Ibid, 200-201.
10. Unger, *Unger's Bible Dictionary,* 1025.
11. Feinberg, *The Sacred Echo,* 169.
12. Greig, *God on Mute,* 226.
13. Feinberg, *The Sacred Echo,* 171.
14. Greig, *God on Mute,* 202.

15. Feinberg, *The Sacred Echo,* 170-183.
16. *Never Doubt*, from the album *Hoping & Coping* by Salmond and Mulder (Image VII, 1981).
17. John Bunyan, *The Pilgrim's Progress* (New York: Penguin Classics, 1987), 138.
18. Lewis, *The Screwtape Letters,* 39.
19. Greig, *God on Mute,* 101-102.

Lesson 13 ~ *Trusting God's Blessings*
1. Charles F. Pfeiffer and Everett F. Harrison, eds., *The Wycliffe Bible Commentary* (Chicago: Moody Press, 1962), 936-7.
2. Greig, *God on Mute,* 144.
3. Janeen Brady, *Standin' Tall* ® *with Gratitude* (Brite Music Enterprises, 1982).
4. Greig, *God on Mute,* 174.

About the Author

Michelle Merrin was raised in a Christian home and came to know Christ as Lord at an early age. After a year at a private secular college, where her faith was challenged and personalized, she completed her education at Seattle Pacific University with a degree in psychology. Michelle met her husband, Ron, at SPU, and they have been happily married for over thirty years.

Her most fulfilling role in life (so far!) was as a fulltime, stay-at-home Mom for nearly twenty-two years for their two sons, Scott and Brad, who are now grown. During this time, she spent many years leading numerous women's Bible studies and serving in various leadership positions within the church. Also a musician, she served in worship ministry for twenty-five years and was a private piano teacher for fifteen years.

Michelle's journey through several difficult life experiences, including infertility, times of unemployment, major health concerns like cancer diagnosis and treatment, and the failure of a business, has challenged and transformed her faith as God has shown himself to be faithful and his grace to be sufficient. She has a passion for God's truth and desires to help others grow spiritually and realize their full spiritual potential. She has written other unpublished Bible studies and also enjoys photography, baking, scrapbooking, computer graphic design, and reading books that are spiritually challenging.

She and Ron reside in Olympia, Washington, and are members of Mt. View Church of the Nazarene in neighboring Tumwater. They enjoy their empty nest but always look forward to the time they get to spend with their children as well.

CPSIA information can be obtained at www.ICGtesting.com
Printed in the USA
LVOW040828270812

296093LV00004B/51/P